大学入試　全レベル問題集　英語長文

レベル6［三訂版］ 別冊（問題編）

目 次

編集部より

問題を解くときには英文音声は必要ありま〔　〕ず，復習の際にはぜひ音声を利用して英文の通し聞きを繰り返しおこなってく〔　〕やイントネーションの定着に，音声を介したインプットは非常に効果〔　〕

ナバホ語（Navajo）に関する次の英文を読んで，4〜5ページの問いに答えなさい。

　　Eugene Crawford is a Navajo, a Native American; he cannot forget the day he and his friends were recruited for the United States military.　Upon arrival at Camp Elliott, they were led to a classroom, which reminded him of the ones he had entered in
5　boarding schools as a child.　Those memories were far from pleasant.　(1)He could almost taste the harsh brown soap the teachers had forced him to use to wash his mouth out when he was caught speaking Navajo.　His thoughts were interrupted when the door suddenly opened and an officer entered.　The new
10　recruits stood to attention.　"At ease, gentlemen.　Please be seated."

　　The first hour they spent in that building changed their lives forever, and the shock of what occurred is still felt by them to this day.　They could never have imagined the project the
15　military had recruited them for.　Some of them believed that, had they known beforehand, they might not have joined up so eagerly. Navajo had been chosen as a code for secret messages because unless you were a Navajo, you'd never understand a word of it. Navajo is a complex language and a slight change in
20　pronunciation can completely change the meaning of a message. The government's decision was wise — it turned out to be the only code the enemy never managed to break — but for the young Navajo soldiers, it was a nightmare.　(2)At no time under any circumstances were they to leave the building without permission
25　or alone.　They were forbidden to tell anyone about the project, even their families, until it was finally made public in 1968.

　　Many of these men had been punished, sometimes brutally, for speaking Navajo in classrooms similar to this, classrooms in

schools run by the same government.　(3)Now this government
³⁰ that had punished them in the past for speaking their own
language was asking them to use it to help win the war. White
people were stranger than the Navajo had imagined.

問 下線部(1)(2)(3)を日本語に訳しなさい。

(1)

(2)

(3)

_____

_____

_____

_____

_____

_____

次の英文を読んで，8～9ページの問いに答えなさい。

　　As we put ever more of our lives into the Cloud and on storage devices like external drives, tablets, and smartphones, we place bits and pieces of our culture there as well: music, art, literature, maps, videos, and photos. These are all artifacts of our culture.　(1)The problem with this data storage is that it is changing all the time and with every significant change there is always the possibility of losing data.　And if you think that (2)keeping it all in the Cloud is the answer, it isn't.　Take a solar flare* as an example.　If a major solar flare wipes out Amazon, Apple, Facebook, and other data centers, all will be lost.　Or if one of these companies goes bankrupt, it is possible that the data it hosts will be lost.　The point is that there are many ways that we could lose our digital culture.

　　Such loss of our digital culture could make it difficult for those in the future to understand how we lived.　This is because (3)it is the small bits and pieces of a culture that we barely think about that often deliver the greatest clues and insights to archeologists and anthropologists studying past cultures.　The materials and process used to make an ancient clay pot, for example, tell us about the food culture of the society that made it. The layout of buildings, to cite another example, can tell us if the society was ruled by a king or queen or if it was more communal. Studying humanity's past helps us navigate today and seek for the future.　Through archeology and anthropology, we've been able to understand different political systems and methods of governance in the past which have informed how we govern our societies today.

　　It is therefore a matter of (　**A**　) that we work to save the artifacts of our digital culture.　We may in the distant future seek

30 to understand at what point and how artificial intelligence came
to （ **B** ）in our societies and how it affected our cultures. We
may want to know how we let social media run amok* and what
（ **C** ）, good and bad, it had on cultures around the world.
Culture is the knowledge we use to navigate our life and world.
35 So the question then becomes, how do we （ **D** ）that our digital
lives and desiderata* are preserved as much as possible? How do
they get copied into new storage formats? Preserving our present
for the future is （ **E** ）for cultural understanding and
navigating our world in the future.

［注＊］　solar flare：太陽面爆発，太陽フレア

run amok：暴走する，手に負えなくなる

desiderata：必要な物，欲しいもの

問1 下線部(1)The problem with this data storage とはどのようなことか，日本語で具体的に述べなさい。

_____

_____

問2 下線部(2)keeping it all in the Cloud にはどのような難点があるか，日本語で具体的に述べなさい。

_____

_____

_____

問3 下線部(3)を日本語に訳しなさい。

_____

_____

問4 (A)〜(E)の空欄に入る最もふさわしい語を以下からそれぞれ1つ選び，その語を書きなさい。

critical   dominate   ensure   impacts   survival

(A)_____   (B)_____   (C)_____

(D)_____   (E)_____

　筆者が文化とは何かについて簡潔にまとめた 1 文を見つけて，その文を
日本語に訳しなさい。

次の英文を読んで，12 〜 13 ページの問いに答えなさい。

　　　　Sailors have long known that whales make strange musical noises. Yet it wasn't until recording techniques were developed that anyone could listen to whale songs （　ア　） their entirety. It was, in fact, military science that first collected the evidence.
5 （　イ　） the Cold War, the US government conducted secret research into how sound travels underwater. The Americans were looking for ways to locate enemy submarines, and to hide their own. They knew that sound travels five times faster underwater than it does through the air, but they also found that
10 it travels at different speeds in different layers of the ocean, fastest of all at the bottom. (1)This may seem surprising, but as David Rothenberg explains: "(2)The denser the medium, the faster the molecules shake as the sound wave goes through it."
　　　　（　ウ　） listening to the ocean, the scientists heard low
15 moaning and rumbling* noises that they gradually learned to identify (and dismiss) as the sound of living creatures. These turned out to be great whales communicating with one another in the deep sound channels, where their utterances travelled （　エ　） hundreds, even thousands of miles.
20 　　　　By listening to humpback whale* songs through underwater microphones, scientists discovered that whales do not cry and moan randomly. The songs — always sung by males — had long-range structures, sometimes lasting for hours. They were shaped like any good musical composition, with themes, phrases,
25 climaxes, resolution*, and dying away. Moreover, the songs were repeated after a pause. They seemed to be transmitted to other whales living in the same area who sang them too. Different groups in other oceans had their own distinctive songs. The songs were too long and formal merely to be passing on simple

³⁰ information about females, food or the ocean floor. Strangest of all, they underwent slow but continuous evolution. Researchers who came back summer after summer noticed subtle changes in the songs each year, all the whales in the area picking up the changes. This means that whales are very different from birds, ³⁵ those other well-known singers of the natural world, whose songs remain stable over time. Whereas today's nightingales may sound very similar to the ones that Shakespeare heard, a whale researcher will complain that the great whale singers of the 1970s have gone now, and that the music favored by today's ⁴⁰ youngsters is entirely different.

(3)<u>Whales became big</u>, so to speak, when endangered species caught our imagination in the 70s. The idea that the world's largest creatures were singing at the bottom of the ocean had great emotional power. Some musicians even went out in ⁴⁵ boats to play to them. Did the whales respond? The musicians thought so. It was all meant to be a homage, an inter-species get-together, but it had to stop when the Marine Mammal Protection Act forbade anyone from harassing the animals and classed music as a form of harassment.

⁵⁰ Some people warn that because of motorized shipping and seismic[*] exploration of the ocean floor by oil companies, the seas are getting much noisier. There is evidence that whales are trying to sing louder to make themselves heard; furthermore, recent sonar tests have been known to kill whales.

⁵⁵ We know that whale songs are complex messages, but we still don't know what they mean or what we could learn from them, and now they may be (　オ　) threat.

[注＊]　moaning and rumbling：うめき，うなる
　　　　humpback whale：ザトウクジラ
　　　　themes, phrases, climaxes, resolution：テーマ，楽句，クライマッ
　　　　　　　　　　　　　　　　　　　　　　　クス，（不協和音の）解決
　　　　seismic：地震(性)の

問1 本文中の(ア)〜(オ)にあてはまる最も適当な語を，①〜⑧から1つ選び，記号で答えなさい(同じ語を二度選んではいけません)。

① across   ② while   ③ against   ④ in

⑤ during   ⑥ at   ⑦ among   ⑧ under

(ア) ☐   (イ) ☐   (ウ) ☐   (エ) ☐   (オ) ☐

問2 本文中の下線部(1)の This が指し示す内容を，日本語でわかりやすく説明しなさい。

_____

_____

問3 本文中の下線部(2)の意味を日本語で表しなさい。

_____

_____

_____

問4 本文では，クジラと鳥はどのような点で異なると述べているか。日本語でわかりやすく説明しなさい。

_____

_____

_____

問5 本文中の下線部(3)に最も近い意味の表現を，①～⑤の中から1つ選び，記号で答えなさい。

① Whales became mature.

② Whales grew larger.

③ Whales' numbers increased.

④ Whales attracted a lot of attention.

⑤ Whales came to live longer.

問6 本文の内容に合うものを①～⑤の中から1つ選び，記号で答えなさい。

① Researchers had long suspected that whales communicated with each other before the recording techniques were fully developed for underwater research.

② Years of intensive research on whale songs uncovered that they are related to mating rituals.

③ Female whales sing in a very different way from male whales.

④ Some musicians intended to harass whales by playing music underwater.

⑤ It is not allowed to play music to whales any more because music is thought to disturb them.

次の英文を読んで，16 〜 17 ページの問いに答えなさい。

(1)Some scientific concepts have been so ruined by our education system that it is necessary to explain the ones that everyone thinks they know about and really don't.

　　We learn about experimentation in school. What we learn is
5 that scientists conduct experiments, and in our high school labs if we copy exactly what they did, we will get the results they got. We learn about the experiments scientists do — usually about the physical and chemical properties of things — and we learn that they report their results in scientific journals. So, in effect, we
10 learn that experimentation is boring, is something done by scientists, and has nothing to do with our daily lives.

　　And (2)this is a problem. Experimentation is something done by everyone all the time. Babies experiment with what might be good to put in their mouths. Toddlers experiment with
15 various behaviors to see what they can get away with. Teenagers experiment with sex, drugs, and rock and roll. But because people don't really see these things as experiments or as ways of collecting evidence in support or refutation of hypotheses*, they don't learn to think about experimentation as something they do
20 constantly and thus need to learn to do better.

　　Every time we take a prescription drug, we are conducting an experiment. But we don't carefully record the results after each dose, and we don't run controlled experiments, and we mix up the variables* by not changing only one behavior at a time, so
25 that when we suffer from side effects we can't figure out what might have been their true cause. We do the same with personal relationships: When they go wrong, we can't figure out why, because the conditions are different in each one.

　　Now, while it is difficult if not impossible to conduct

30 controlled experiments in most aspects of our lives, it is possible
to come to understand that we are indeed conducting an
experiment when we take a new job, or try a new tactic in a
game, or pick a school to attend — or when we try and figure out
how someone is feeling or wonder why we ourselves feel as we do.
35 　　　Every aspect of life is an experiment that can be better
understood if it is perceived in that way.　But because we don't
recognize this, we fail to understand that we need to reason
logically from evidence we gather, carefully consider the
conditions under which our experiment has been conducted, and
40 decide when and how we might run the experiment again with
better results.　　The scientific activity that surrounds
experimentation is about thinking clearly in the face of evidence
obtained from the experiment.　(3)But people who don't see their
actions as experiments and don't know how to reason carefully
45 from data will continue to learn less well from their experiences
than those who do.
　　　Most of us, having learned the word "experiment" in the
context of a boring ninth-grade science class, have long since
learned to discount science and experimentation as irrelevant to
50 our lives.　If schools taught basic cognitive* concepts, such as
experimentation in the context of everyday experience, instead of
concentrating on algebra* as a way of teaching people how to
reason, then people would be much more effective at thinking
about politics, child raising, personal relationships, business, and
55 every other aspect of their daily lives.

　[注＊]　　refutation of hypotheses：仮説の反証
　　　　　variables：変数
　　　　　cognitive：認知に関する，認知的な
　　　　　algebra：代数

15

問 1 下線部(1)を和訳しなさい。

問 2 下線部(2)の具体的な内容を，句読点を含め，60 字以内で述べなさい。

60字

問 3 下線部(3)を和訳しなさい。

問4 処方薬を飲んで副作用が出た場合，その原因を知るために私たちはどのようにすべきだと筆者は考えているか。句読点を含め，60字以内で述べなさい。

60字

次の英文を読んで，20 ～ 21 ページの問いに答えなさい。

　　　It has long been thought that one of the characteristics which separate humans from other animals is the ability to reason. Whereas animals are slaves to their instincts, such as hunger, thirst, fear and the need to reproduce, humans have the
5 capacity to control their urges and reflect upon their feelings. Promotion of the use of reason was central to the Enlightenment movement in 18th century Europe. The ability to think problems through logically is something on which Western civilizations have prided themselves. However, while it is certainly true that
10 humans possess the capacity to employ logic in problem solving and in making good decisions, psychologists have shown in experimental studies that humans are likely to act irrationally far more often than is commonly perceived.

　　　One example of (1)this is the influence of words. If you
15 have recently read or heard someone say the word 'eat', then you will be more likely to use a 'u' rather than an 'a' to fill in the blank in the combination: 'so_p'. You will also be better able to recognize the word 'soup' when 'soup' is whispered to you than if you had not just been exposed to the idea of 'eating'. Words can
20 also influence our physical actions. In a famous experiment, a group of American university students were told to make a sentence using a set of words presented to them. They were divided into two groups. One group was given a word list containing words which are normally associated with the elderly,
25 such as 'retirement', 'wrinkle', 'grey', 'slow' and 'pension', while the list given to the other group contained no such words. When the students had finished their task, they were told to change rooms. The researchers found that the students who had been working with the set of words associated with old age walked

³⁰ more slowly than the other group. The word 'old' was not used, and all the students said in the interview after the experiment that they were unaware of (2)<u>the theme</u> suggested by the words. Their behaviour had been influenced unconsciously.

   The phenomenon described above is known in psychology as ³⁵ 'priming'. It can also be produced through your own gestures. This is because gestures are also a form of communication. For example, nodding means 'yes' and shaking the head means 'no'. To demonstrate how 'priming' may also apply to gestures, American university students in another experiment were given ⁴⁰ a set of headphones to wear. An opinion taken from a radio show was played through the headphones and the students were instructed to check for sound problems by moving their heads. Half of the students were asked to nod their heads up and down, while (**3**) half were asked to shake their heads from side to ⁴⁵ side. The experimenters found that (4)<u>the students who nodded their heads up and down were more likely to agree with the opinion which they had heard through the headphones</u>. This contrasted with the group that shook their heads, who were more likely to disagree.

⁵⁰   While no one would argue that humans are completely irrational, we are open to suggestion far more than we would like to believe. We should therefore be aware of this when taking important decisions, especially if someone is actively trying to influence the outcome, such as in advertizing, or even when in ⁵⁵ supermarkets. For example, the interiors of these shops are often designed by psychologists to encourage what is known as 'impulse buying'. The use of lighting to display certain products and the physical placement of goods are designed with (5)<u>this aim</u> in mind. It is no accident that comfort foods such as sweets and ⁶⁰ chocolates are frequently displayed at the checkout counter, where people have to wait in line. It may be impossible to make ourselves immune to all suggestion, but a little self-reflection before we act may (6)<u>go a long way</u>.

問1 下線部(1)が表す内容を日本語で述べなさい。

_____

_____

_____

問2 下線部(2)が指している内容を表す語句を，次の①〜④の中から1つ選び，記号で答えなさい。

① our physical actions   ② the elderly

③ the influence of words   ④ unconsciousness

```
┌──────┐
│      │
└──────┘
```

問3 空欄(3)に入る最も適切な語句を，次の①〜④の中から1つ選び，記号で答えなさい。

① another   ② other   ③ the another   ④ the other

```
┌──────┐
│      │
└──────┘
```

問4 下線部(4)の理由を，本文に即して，60字以内の日本語で述べなさい。

60字

問5 下線部(5)が指している内容を日本語で具体的に述べなさい。

_____

_____

問6 下線部(6)の意味に最も近い意味をもつ語句を，次の①〜④の中から1つ選び，記号で答えなさい。

① be helpful　② be possible　③ know better　④ take some time

□

問7 本文の内容と合致<u>しない</u>ものを，次の①〜⑥の中から2つ選び，記号で答えなさい。

① Almost every aspect of human behaviour is actually controlled by instinctive urges.

② Contemporary people think they are far more rational than people in the 18th century.

③ People are readily affected by subtle signals that are not very explicit.

④ You can recognize words more easily when some related words have been presented to you beforehand.

⑤ Your physical actions may influence your attitude toward an opinion you hear.

⑥ Western Europeans in the 18th century strongly believed in the power of human reason.

□　□

次の英文は，"Why can some fish live in freshwater, some in salt water, and some in　both?" と題された記事である。これを読んで，24 ～ 25 ページの問いに答えなさい。

　　The various species of fish found in oceans, lakes, rivers and streams have evolved over millions of years and have adapted to their preferred environments over long periods of time. Fish are categorized according to their (1)salinity tolerance. Fish that can
5 tolerate only very narrow ranges of salinity (such freshwater fish as goldfish and such saltwater fish as tuna) are known as stenohaline species. These fish die in waters having a salinity that differs from that in their natural environments.

　　Fish that can tolerate a wide range of salinity at some phase
10 in their life-cycle are called euryhaline species. These fish, which include salmon, eels, and striped bass, can live or survive in wide ranges of salinity, varying from fresh to brackish to marine waters. A period of gradual adjustment, though, may be needed for euryhaline fish to tolerate large changes in salinity.

15 　　It is believed that when the newly formed planet Earth cooled sufficiently, rain began to fall continuously. This rainfall filled the first oceans with fresh water. (2)It was the constant evaporation of water from the ocean that then condensed to cause rainfall on the land, which in turn, caused the ocean to become
20 salty over several billion years. As rain water washed over and through the soil, it dissolved many minerals — sodium, potassium* and calcium — and carried them back to the ocean.

　　Vertebrate animals* (fish, birds, mammals, reptiles and amphibians) have a unique and common characteristic. The salt
25 content of their blood is virtually identical. Vertebrate blood has a salinity of approximately 9 grams per liter (a 0.9 percent salt solution). Almost 77 percent of the salts in blood are sodium and

chloride*. The remainder is made up primarily of bicarbonate, potassium and calcium. Sodium, potassium and calcium salts are critical for the normal function of heart, nerve and muscle tissue.

If the salinity of ocean water is diluted to approximately one quarter of its normal concentration, it has almost the same salinity as fish blood and contains similar proportions of sodium, potassium, calcium and chloride. The similarities between the salt content of vertebrate blood and dilute seawater suggest a strong evolutionary relationship among vertebrates and with the ancient oceans.

Indeed, it seems likely that vertebrate life evolved when the ocean was approximately one quarter as salty as it is today. As the ocean became saltier and vertebrates evolved further, several groups of vertebrates (birds, mammals, reptiles and amphibians) left the ocean to inhabit the land, carrying the seawater with them as their blood. They maintained their blood salt concentrations by drinking freshwater and absorbing salts from food.

But fish stayed in the aquatic environment. To adapt, they had to either remain in low salinity environments, such as bays and estuaries*, or they had to evolve mechanisms to replace water lost through osmosis* to the seawater and to remove salts absorbed from the increasingly saline oceans. To inhabit fresh water, fish had to replace salts lost through diffusion* to the water and eliminate excess water absorbed from the environment. Kidney function had to be altered accordingly for fish to survive in these different habitats. Eventually, the gills* developed the ability to excrete* salts in seawater and absorb salts from fresh water.

In seawater, fish must drink salt water to replace lost fluids and then eliminate the excess salts. Their kidneys produce small volumes of fluid containing high concentrations of salt. Freshwater fish produce large volumes of dilute urine, which is

low in salt. High concentrations of environmental calcium help reduce salt loss through the gills and body surfaces in freshwater environments. Less demand is placed on the kidneys to maintain stable concentrations of blood salts in brackish or low salinity
65 waters.

Ultimately, fish adapted to or inhabited marine, fresh or brackish water because each environment offered (3)<u>some competitive advantage</u> to the different species. For instance, it has been suggested that euryhaline fish are able to eliminate
70 external parasites by moving to and from fresh and saltwaters. Habitats of wide ranges of salinity offered new or more food, escape from predators and even stable temperatures.

［注＊］　potassium：カリウム　　　　vertebrate animal：脊椎動物
　　　　　chloride：塩化物　　　　　　estuary：河口
　　　　　osmosis：浸透　　　　　　　diffusion：拡散
　　　　　gill：えら　　　　　　　　　excrete：排出する

問1　下線部(1)は何を意味しているか，本文に即して<u>日本語</u>で説明しなさい。

_____

_____

問2　下線部(2)を日本語に訳しなさい。

_____

_____

_____

_____

問3 下線部(3)について，本文であげられているすべての具体例を，日本語で述べなさい。

_____

_____

_____

_____

問4 本文によれば，脊椎動物には，どのような要因で，どのような進化が起こったか。英語で要約しなさい。

_____

_____

_____

_____

_____

_____

_____

_____

次の英文を読んで，28 〜 29 ページの問いに答えなさい。(*を付した語句には，問題文の末尾に注がある。)

　　　Green may not be the most fashionable color this spring, but it's still popular among many travelers.　A survey found that 58 percent of hotel guests preferred staying at an environmentally friendly property.　Nearly 40 percent said
5　they're willing to spend an extra $10 a night to sleep at a sustainable* resort.　If you're a hotel manager, hanging a sign on your door that says you're green — even if you aren't — can increase profits.　A study found that 60 percent of U.S. travelers have taken a "sustainable" trip in the last three years and that
10　these travelers spend on average $600 per trip, and stay three days longer than the average guest.　The expanding green-travel market is now "too big to ignore."

　　　Yet some travelers remain unsure about green travel.　"For me, green implies no manufactured products," says a frequent
15　traveler.　And by that standard, no airplane, cruise ship, or hotel can truly be considered green.　In a perfect world, for a hotel to be considered green, it would have to be completely demolished, and trees would have to be planted over it.　And then people would let nature take its (　**A**　).　But that's not the world we live in.
20　Still, at a time when terms like "green," "sustainable," and "environmentally friendly" are used too much — often with the intent of convincing you to make a travel plan — it's worth asking how to separate real green from fake green.

　　　An eco-travel specialist advises travelers to do your research
25　to determine whether green travel options are legitimate.　For example, many hotels promote their Leadership in Energy and Environmental Design (LEED) certification* from the U.S. Green Building Council, which judges on criteria such as water savings,

energy efficiency, and building material selection. But if you
30 travel abroad, you'll need to be aware of other sustainability-
certification programs, such as Australia's EarthCheck or
Britain's Green Tourism Business Scheme. Hotel chains
sometimes have their own sustainability standards.
InterContinental Hotels Group, which owns the Holiday Inn and
35 Crowne Plaza brands, runs an internal program called "IHG
Green Engage" that lets its hotels measure their environmental
impact. Owners can view reports on water use and utility
consumption with an eye toward reducing their carbon and water
waste.

40   (1)<u>When it comes to airlines and cruise ship companies,
there's a consensus among experts that there's almost no such
thing as green — only shades of fake green.</u> It's said that there's
a lot of greenwashing* and both airplanes and cruise ship
companies pollute to such an extent that some travelers find it
45 difficult to justify a reservation.

It can be even more difficult to assess tours that combine air
travel, hotel stays, and sightseeing into a single package because
of their many components. It's not always easy to tell apart
authentic green, eco-friendly, and sustainable tours from fakes.
50 The best advice is to contact your travel agent and ask some
detailed questions. Those include: What hotels do you prefer to
send your travelers to and why? What common travel practices
do you see that you don't like? How do you operate in a more eco-
friendly way? By making a little bit of extra effort and asking the
55 right questions, you can increase the likelihood that you are
dealing with someone who shares your values.

Aside from what light bulbs they use, how many recycling
boxes you see, or whether they give you the option to decline daily
room service, it's hard to tell at first sight how sustainable a hotel
60 is really trying to be. You'd better see where they are obtaining
their food, what they do with leftovers, and what cleaning

products they use. If you don't like the answers or if they seem (**B**), go elsewhere. Simply stating that they are green or eco-friendly does not guarantee that they are not greenwashing.

65   You need to (2)"dig deep" on a hotel's website to determine things such as the materials used to create the building, its efforts to save fuel and water, and green certifications. If that information is missing, perhaps the hotel's commitment to sustainability just isn't there.

70   No travel agency will come up (**C**). After all, every airplane, cruise ship, hotel, and resort pollutes the environment. Perhaps the best travelers can hope for is that (3)their preference for sustainability will make the industry more responsive to their concerns. Because, in the end, the only thing the travel industry
75 probably cares about is your money.

[注＊]　sustainable：環境に負荷のかからない(sustainability はその名詞形)
　　　　Leadership in Energy and Environmental Design (LEED) certification：アメリカ合衆国の建物の環境性能に関する認証
　　　　greenwash：(企業が)環境問題に関心があるふりをする

問1　下線部(1)を和訳しなさい。

_____

_____

問2　下線部(2)の "dig deep" と同じ意味で使われている３語から成る語句を本文中より書き出しなさい。

_____

問3 下線部(3)のような効果をもたらすために消費者が取るべきと筆者が考える行動を，80字以内の日本語（句読点を含む）で説明しなさい。

80字

問4 空欄（ **A** ）〜（ **C** ）に入れる語として最も適切なものをそれぞれ以下の選択肢①〜④から1つずつ選びなさい。

(A) ① act ② care ③ course ④ drive

(B) ① engaged ② fascinating ③ persuasive ④ suspicious

(C) ① absent ② distant ③ entire ④ perfect

次の英文を読んで，33 ～ 35 ページの問いに答えなさい。

The brain is often envisioned as something like a computer, and the body as its all-purpose tool. But a growing body of new research suggests that something more collaborative is going on — that we think not just with our brains, but with our bodies. A
5 recent series of studies has shown that children can solve math problems better if they are told to use their hands while thinking. Another recent study suggested that stage actors remember their lines better when they are moving. And in one study published last year, (1)a group of people asked to move their eyes in a
10 specific pattern while puzzling through a logical problem were twice as likely to solve it.

The term most often used to describe this new model of mind is "embodied cognition," and its champions believe it will open up entire new avenues for understanding — and enhancing —
15 the abilities of the human mind. Some educators see in (2)it a new paradigm for teaching children, one that privileges movement and simulation over reading, writing, and reciting. Specialists in rehabilitative medicine could potentially use the emerging findings to （　ア　） patients recover lost skills after a
20 stroke or other brain injury. The greatest impact, however, has been in the field of neuroscience itself, where embodied cognition threatens age-old distinctions — not only between brain and body, but between perceiving and thinking, thinking and acting, even between reason and instinct — on which the traditional idea
25 of the mind has been built.

"It's a revolutionary idea," says Shaun Gallagher, the director of the cognitive science program at the University of Central Florida. "In the embodied view, if you're going to explain cognition it's not enough just to look inside the brain. In any

30 particular instance, (3)what's going on inside the brain in large part may depend on what's going on in the body as a whole, and how that body is situated in its environment."

Or, as the motto of the University of Wisconsin's Laboratory of Embodied Cognition puts it, *Ago ergo cogito*: "I act, therefore I 35 think."

The emerging field builds on decades of research into human movement and gesture. Much of the earlier work looked at the role of gestures in communication, asking whether gesture grew out of speech or exploring why people gestured when they 40 were talking on the telephone.

But today, neuroscientists, linguists, and philosophers are making much bolder claims. A few argue that human characteristics like empathy, or concepts like time and space, or even the deep structure of language and some of the most 45 profound principles of mathematics, can ultimately be traced to the idiosyncrasies* of the human body. They argue that (4)if we didn't walk upright or weren't warm-blooded, we might understand these concepts totally differently. The experience of having a body, they argue, is intimately tied to our intelligence.

50 "If you want to (イ) a computer to play chess, or if you want to design a search engine, the old model is OK," says Rolf Pfeifer, director of the artificial intelligence lab at the University of Zurich, "but if you're interested in understanding real intelligence, you have to deal with the body."

55 Embodied cognition upends* several centuries of thinking about thinking. René Descartes*, living in an age when steam engines were novelty items, envisioned the brain as a pump that moved "animating fluid" through the body — head-shrinkers* through the ages have tended to enlist the high-tech of their day 60 to (ウ) the human cognitive system — but the mind, Descartes argued, was something else entirely, an incorporeal* entity that interacted with the body through the pineal gland*.

    While a few thinkers challenged Descartes' mind-body separation, it remained the dominant model up through the 20th
65 century, though its form evolved with the times.   After the development of the modern computer in the years after World War II, a new version of the same model was adopted, with the brain as a computer and the mind as the software that ran on it.
    In the 1980s, however, a group of scholars began to (エ   )
70 this approach.   Fueled in part by broad disappointment with artificial intelligence research, they argued that (5)human beings don't really process information the way computers do, by manipulating abstract symbols using formal rules.   In 1995, a major biological discovery brought even more enthusiasm to the
75 field. Scientists in Italy discovered "mirror neurons" that respond when we see someone else performing an action — or even when we hear an action described — as if we ourselves were performing the action.   By simultaneously playing a role in both acting and thinking, mirror neurons suggested that the two might not be so
80 separate after all.

[注＊]   idiosyncrasy：特質，特異性

        upend：ひっくり返す

        René Descartes：ルネ・デカルト（フランスの哲学者・数学者）

        head-shrinker：精神科医

        incorporeal：実体のない，無形の
        pineal gland：松果腺，松果体

問1 下線部(1)を日本語に訳しなさい。

_____

_____

_____

_____

問2 下線部(2)の it が示す最も適切な連続した 5 語を本文中から英語で抜き出しなさい。

_____

問3 下線部(3)を日本語に訳しなさい。

_____

_____

_____

_____

_____

問 4　下線部(4)を日本語に訳しなさい。

問 5　下線部(5)を日本語に訳しなさい。

問6 空欄(ア)～(エ)に入る最も適切な単語の組み合わせを，①～⑥から1つ選び，記号で答えなさい。

① (ア)teach 　　(イ)help 　　　(ウ)describe 　(エ)contest

② (ア)help 　　(イ)describe 　(ウ)contest 　(エ)teach

③ (ア)contest 　(イ)teach 　　(ウ)help 　　　(エ)describe

④ (ア)describe (イ)help 　　　(ウ)contest 　(エ)teach

⑤ (ア)help 　　(イ)contest 　(ウ)teach 　　(エ)describe

⑥ (ア)help 　　(イ)teach 　　(ウ)describe 　(エ)contest

次の英文を読んで，39 〜 41 ページの問いに答えなさい。

Over the centuries, the credentials needed to carry out scientific research have been in flux. Only recently has science become an occupation. (1)In earlier days, science was something for those with the luxury to dedicate their leisure time or
5 spiritual time to follow their curiosity. In the 1600s, Antonie van Leeuwenhoek discovered microorganisms. His professional background? A cloth merchant who learned to make excellent lenses to judge the weave of fabrics. Eventually, he made lenses more powerful than microscopes at that time, which allowed him
10 to curiously examine mucky pond water and plaque on teeth and find tiny life, earning him the title of father of microbiology. Gregor Mendel filled many of his days as a monk with experimental breeding of pea plants to understand how traits are hereditary. That earned him the title of father of genetics.
15 Charles Darwin was a companion to Captain FitzRoy of the Beagle with time to see the world before planning to return and become a parson. Darwin's later days were part of a shift in science. Not only was science becoming a profession, the precursor to citizen science was beginning: Darwin and others
20 started crowdsourcing for data through letters in which people shared their observations from around the world.

In more recent history, fellow citizen scientists have continued to accomplish the remarkable. Citizen science has contributed hugely to entomology. The mystery of monarch
25 butterfly migration had long eluded scientists until Fred Urquhart and Norah Patterson began experimenting with techniques to affix unique tags to butterflies. Once these scientists identified a way to attach a tag to the butterfly without harming their sensitive wings, (2)可能な限り多くの蝶に彼らがタグ

₃₀ を付けるのを手伝うためには，より多くの人々が必要であることに彼ら
は気がついた． In 1952, they asked for the help of thousands of
volunteers and started a monarch tagging program, which
eventually became the modern-day Monarch Watch. Then, in the
mid-1970s, the first tagged monarch was spotted in Mexico. It
₃₅ turned out to be tagged by a Minnesota* school teacher and two
of his teenage students, which led to the discovery of the long-
distance monarch migration from North America to Mexico in the
fall and the return in the spring. The breakthrough was possible
because thousands of volunteers had been capturing and tagging
₄₀ the wings of monarchs with postage-stamp-size stickers for
decades. To this day people continue to tag monarchs and bring
more discoveries, like making us aware of their current
population decline.

The modern environmental movement was also inspired by
₄₅ citizen scientists. Rachel Carson's seminal book, Silent Spring,
revealed the dangers of the pesticide DDT. Predatory birds, such
as peregrine falcons, became endangered species because DDT
thinned their eggshells. The discovery that their eggshells were
thinning was possible because egg specimens found in museums
₅₀ had thicker eggshells. Non-professionals — citizen scientists —
had collected those eggshells before the manufacturing of DDT
began. (The hobby of collecting wild bird eggs was outlawed in
the United States in 1916 with the Migratory Bird Treaty Act,
which protected migratory birds, including their nests and eggs.)

₅₅   (3)In the mid-1990s, citizen science was key to climate
change negotiations. British scientists found that birds were
laying their eggs earlier in the year because of climate change.
The entire dataset, with hundreds of thousands of nesting
records, was the result of decades of observations by birdwatchers
₆₀ scattered across England. In making the case for the Kyoto
Protocol (the international treaty about climate change action),
the British government relied on that research to show that

climate change was not a "future" problem but a "now" or urgent problem because it was already affecting life on Earth.

65   Today, with the internet and smartphones, <u>science is in flux again</u>. Millions of people, each with their own occupation (and many too young to have an occupation yet), share their observations and help process data. Volunteers work online to transcribe thousands of old letters, some originating with Darwin,
70 others from Shakespeare, and others from war diaries. People are needed to turn handwriting into digital text because automation with optical recognition software can't decipher handwriting as well as the human eye. Today, fields like biochemistry advance because people use their free time as
75 players in online games because the human mind is better at spatial reasoning than computers. In the Eterna game, players design RNA, the blueprints that make proteins. In Foldit, a game to solve puzzles of how proteins fold, some players discovered the folded shape of a particular protein associated with AIDS in
80 monkeys. As environmental and health sensors like Fitbits and air-quality monitors become lower cost, people without science credentials are assessing the quality of their environment, providing a check on industries to make sure regulations are followed. In ports like Oakland, California, with significant truck
85 traffic, and in New Orleans, Louisiana, with petrochemical refineries, communities organized by the West Oakland Environmental Indicators Project and Louisiana Bucket Brigade have discovered excessive exposures to pollution where scientists and regulatory enforcers have failed to look. Across the world,
90 eyes of citizen scientists have discovered that endangered monk seals were attempting to recolonize the Mediterranean Sea, that invasive ladybirds in England were rapidly expanding their range, and three new species of dancing peacock spiders in Australia.

95   Looking across history, (4)<u>what's revealed is that in many</u>

areas of study the only way to keep advancing the frontiers is for scientists to collaborate, not just with each other, but with everyone.

［注＊］　Minnesota：アメリカ合衆国内陸の北部にある州の１つ

問1　下線部(1)を日本語に訳しなさい。

_____

_____

問2　下線部(2)を英語に訳しなさい。

_____

_____

問3　下線部(3)に関連して，京都議定書(Kyoto Protocol)をめぐるイギリス政府の交渉において市民科学が果たした役割とその意義とは何か。60字以内の日本語で説明しなさい。（句読点も文字数に含める。）

60字

問4　下線部(4)を日本語に訳しなさい。

_____

_____

以下の(1)と(2)の答えとして最も適切なものを，(1)については①〜⑦，(2)については①〜⑤の中から選び，番号で答えなさい。

(1) According to paragraph 3, in which order did the following events happen? Choose one from ① to ⑦.

A Rachael Carson published Silent Spring.

B Predatory birds faced a crisis because of their thinned eggshells.

C Citizen scientists legally gathered eggshell samples.

D The pesticide DDT was manufactured.

① A→B→C→D   ② A→C→D→B   ③ B→A→C→D

④ B→C→D→A   ⑤ C→B→D→A   ⑥ C→D→B→A

⑦ D→B→C→A

(2) Look at the double underlined part in paragraph 5. What does the author mean by "science is in flux again"? Choose one from ① to ⑤.

① A traditional scientific approach is considered particularly important in assessing new surroundings or environments.

② Citizen scientists today are significantly affecting the world of science like their predecessors did.

③ It happens that the history of science is more often than not marked by images of water.

④ Scientists are constantly facing problems that have arisen over and over again in human history.

⑤ Scientists are reluctant to accept ideas from different occupations to create new theories.

問6 次の①～⑦の文から，本文の内容に一致するものを２つ選び，番号で答えなさい。

① Antonie van Leeuwenhoek encouraged his fellow citizen scientists to make science their profession as he dedicated his life to lens making and microorganisms.

② A Minnesota school teacher and two of his teenage students reported evidence that monarch butterflies travel from North America to Mexico.

③ Tagging monarchs has led to an understanding of their migration patterns and an awareness of their decline in numbers.

④ Citizen scientists meet online to translate letters written by Darwin and Shakespeare.

⑤ Computers go beyond human capacity for spatial reasoning, efficiently analyzing handwritten letters and proteins.

⑥ Health monitors can record the quality of air, detect protein folding, and provide detailed data for the advancement of science.

⑦ Observations by citizen scientists have led to discoveries of new species and brought to light behaviors of endangered sea animals.

次の英文（『世界開発報告 2019 年版』の冒頭部分）を読み，46 〜 47 ページの問いに日本語で答えなさい。この世界銀行の報告書には毎年テーマが設定されており，この年のテーマは The Changing Nature of Work であった。

[1] There has never been a time when mankind was not afraid of where its talent for innovation might lead. In the 19th century, Karl Marx worried that "machinery does not just act as a superior competitor to the worker, always on the point of making him
5 superfluous*. It is the most powerful weapon for suppressing* strikes." John Maynard Keynes warned in 1930 of widespread unemployment arising from technology. And yet innovation has transformed living standards. Life expectancy has gone up; basic health care and education are widespread; and most people have
10 seen their incomes rise.

[2] Three-quarters of the citizens of the European Union, the world's lifestyle superpower, believe that the workplace benefits from technology, according to a recent Eurobarometer* survey. Two-thirds said technology will benefit society and improve their
15 quality of life even further.

[3] Despite this optimism, concerns about the future remain. People living in advanced economies are anxious about the sweeping* impact of technology on employment. They hold a view that rising inequality, compounded* by the advent* of the
20 gig economy (in which organizations contract with independent workers for short-term engagements), is encouraging a race to the bottom* in working conditions.

[4] This troubling scenario, however, is on balance unfounded. It is true that in some advanced economies and middle-income
25 countries manufacturing jobs are being lost to automation. Workers undertaking routine tasks that are "codifiable*" are the most vulnerable* to replacement. And yet technology provides opportunities to create new jobs, increase productivity, and

deliver effective public services. Through innovation, technology
30 generates new sectors and new tasks.
[5]   Some features of the current wave of technological progress
are notable. Digital technologies allow firms to scale up or down
quickly, blurring* the boundaries of firms and challenging
traditional production patterns. New business models — digital
35 platform firms — are evolving from local start-ups to global
behemoths*, often with few employees or tangible assets. This
new industrial organization poses policy questions in the areas of
privacy, competition, and taxation. The ability of governments to
raise revenues is curtailed by the virtual nature of productive
40 assets.
[6]   The rise of platform marketplaces allows the effects of
technology to reach more people more quickly than ever before.
Individuals and firms need only a broadband connection to trade
goods and services on online platforms. This "scale without mass"
45 brings economic opportunity to millions of people who do not live
in industrialized countries or even industrial areas.   The
changing demand for skills reaches the same people. Automation
raises the premium on high-order cognitive* skills in advanced
and emerging economies.
50 [7]   Investing in human capital is the priority to make the most
of this evolving economic opportunity. Three types of skills are
increasingly important in labor markets: advanced cognitive
skills such as complex problem-solving, sociobehavioral skills
such as teamwork, and skill combinations that are predictive* of
55 adaptability such as reasoning and self-efficacy*. Building these
skills requires strong human capital foundations and lifelong
learning.
[8]   The foundations of human capital, created in early
childhood, have thus become more important. Yet governments
60 in developing countries do not give priority to early childhood
development, and the human capital outcomes of basic schooling

are suboptimal. The World Bank's new human capital index, presented in this study for the first time, highlights the link between investments in health and education and the
65 productivity of future workers. For example, climbing from the 25th to the 75th percentile on the index brings an additional 1.4 percent annual growth over 50 years.

[9]   Creating formal jobs is the first-best policy, consistent with the International Labour Organization's decent work agenda, to
70 seize the benefits of technological change. In many developing countries, most workers remain in low-productivity employment, often in the informal sector* with little access to technology. Lack of quality private sector jobs leaves talented young people with few pathways to wage employment. High-skill university
75 graduates currently make up almost 30 percent of the unemployed pool of labor in the Middle East and North Africa. Better adult learning opportunities enable those who have left school to reskill according to changing labor market demands.

[10] Investments in infrastructure are also needed. Most
80 obvious are investments in affordable access to the Internet for people in developing countries who remain unconnected. Equally important are more investments in the road, port, and municipal infrastructure on which firms, governments, and individuals rely to exploit technologies to their full potential.

85 [11] Adjusting to the next wave of jobs requires social protection. Eight in 10 people in developing countries receive no social assistance, and 6 in 10 work informally without insurance.

[12] Even in advanced economies, the payroll-based insurance model is increasingly challenged by working arrangements
90 outside standard employment contracts. What are some new ways of protecting people? A societal minimum* that provides support independent of employment is one option. This model, which would include mandated and voluntary social insurance, could reach many more people.

₉₅ [13] Social protection can be strengthened by expanding overall coverage that prioritizes the neediest people in society. Placing community health workers on the government's payroll* is a step in the right direction. A universal basic income is another possibility, but it is untested and fiscally prohibitive for emerging ₁₀₀ economies. Enhanced social assistance and insurance systems would reduce the burden of risk management on labor regulation. As people become better protected through such systems, labor regulation could, where appropriate, be made more balanced to facilitate* movement between jobs.

₁₀₅ [14] For societies to benefit from the potential that technology offers, they would need (1)a new social contract centered on larger investments in human capital and progressively provided universal social protection. However, social inclusion requires fiscal space, and many developing countries lack the finances ₁₁₀ because of inadequate tax bases, large informal sectors, and inefficient administration.

[15] And yet there is plenty of room for improvement through, for example, better collection of property taxes in urban municipalities or the introduction of excise taxes* on sugar or ₁₁₅ tobacco. The latter would have direct health benefits as well. Levying* indirect taxes, reforming subsidies, and reducing tax avoidance by global corporations, especially among the new platform companies, are other possible sources of financing. (2)In fact, the traditional structure of the global tax order provides ₁₂₀ opportunities for multinational corporations to engage in base erosion and profit shifting — that is, some firms allocate more profits to affiliates located in zero- or low-tax countries no matter how little business is conducted there. By some estimates, on average, 50 percent of the total foreign income of multinationals ₁₂₅ is reported in jurisdictions* with an effective tax rate of less than 5 percent.

[16] Emerging economies are in the middle of a technological

shift that is bringing change to the nature of work. Whatever the
future holds, investment in human capital is a no-regrets policy
130 that prepares people for the challenges ahead.

[注＊] 　advent：出現，到来　　behemoth：ビヒモス（聖書にでてくる巨獣），巨大
なもの　　blur：あいまいにする，ぼんやりさせる　　codifiable：成文化可
能な　　cognitive：認識力にかかわる　　compound：混ぜ合わせる
Eurobarometer：ユーロバロメーター，EU の世論調査
excise taxes：物品税，消費税　　facilitate：促進する，容易にする
informal　sector：インフォーマル・セクター　　jurisdiction：法的権限の
管轄区域，法域　　levy：課税する，課する　　payroll：給与支払い対象者
名簿　　predictive of ～：～の前兆となる，～を予想させる
race to the bottom：底辺への競争（過度な競争の結果，全員の環境や条件が
悪化すること）　　self-efficacy：自己効力感，何かを達成できるという自信
societal　minimum：社会的ミニマム，社会的最低基準　　superfluous：余
分な，不必要な　　suppress：抑圧する　　sweeping：一掃するような，広
範囲にわたる　　vulnerable：脆弱な，弱みがある

問1 　この文章の内容は，６つのブロック（かたまり）に分けることができ，最
も適切な「区切り方」と各ブロックの「小見出し」を次の表に整理した。
「区切り方」欄のカッコ内に，当てはまる段落番号を記入後，「小見出し」
欄のカッコ内に，〈小見出しの候補群〉のうち，最も適切な語句の丸数字
を記入し，表を完成させなさい。

ブロック名	区切り方	各ブロックの小見出し
第Ⅰブロック	第１段落から第（　）段落まで	（　　　）
第Ⅱブロック	第（　）段落から第９段落まで	（　　　）
第Ⅲブロック	第 10 段落	（　　　）
第Ⅳブロック	第 11 段落から第（　）段落まで	（　　　）
第Ⅴブロック	第（　）段落から第 15 段落まで	（　　　）
第Ⅵブロック	第 16 段落	②

「区切り方」は，第Ⅲブロックを第 10 段落，第Ⅳブロックを第 16 段
落とし，「小見出し」については，最後の第Ⅵブロックを②とする。
〈小見出しの候補群〉には，該当しない選択肢が３つ含まれている。

〈小見出しの候補群〉
① Community health workers
② Conclusions
③ Economics and business management
④ Impacts of new technologies and innovation
⑤ Investing in education and creating formal jobs
⑥ Investing in infrastructure
⑦ New social contract
⑧ Public policies of local governments
⑨ Social protection

問2 下線部(1)の a new social contract は何を意味し，その実現のために
は何が必要かを文意に即して日本語で説明しなさい。

_____

_____

_____

問3 下線部(2)を日本語に訳しなさい。なお，base erosion は「税源の浸食」
と訳しなさい。

_____

_____

_____

出典一覧：

英文 1：From *Navajo Weapon: The Navajo Code Talkers* by Sally McClain, pages 49-51. Copyright © 2002. Reprinted by permission of Rio Nuevo Publishers.

英文 2：*In Our Digital Future, Will We Lose Our History?* by Giles Crouch (digital anthropologist). Reproduced by permission.

英文 3：*Deep-sea groover* by Susan Tomes, Copyright Guardian News & Media Ltd, 2015.

英文 4："Experimentation" by Roger Schank [pp. 23-24: 600 words] from *This Will Make You Smarter* by John Brockman. Copyright © 2012 by Edge Foundation, Inc. Reprinted by permission of HarperCollins Publishers.

英文 5：北海道大学

英文 6：*Why can some fish live in freshwater, some in salt water, and some in both?* By William A. Wurts from World Aquaculture vol.29 issue 1. ©1998 World Aquaculture Society.

英文 7：Used with permission of Washington Post News Media Services, from *With eco-friendly travel more popular than ever, approach green claims with skepticism* by Christopher Elliott; permission conveyed through Copyright Clearance Center, Inc.

英文 8：*Don't Just Stand There, Think* by Drake Bennett. From The Boston Globe, January 13 © 2008 Boston Globe Media Partners. All rights reserved. Used under license.

英文 9：From *The Field Guide to Citizen Science* by Darlene Cavalier, copyright ©2020. Reprinted by permission of Timber, an imprint of Hachette Book Group, Inc.

英文 10：横浜国立大学

学ぶ人は、
変えて
ゆく人だ。

目の前にある問題はもちろん、

人生の問いや、

社会の課題を自ら見つけ、

挑み続けるために、人は学ぶ。

「学び」で、

少しずつ世界は変えてゆける。

いつでも、どこでも、誰でも、

学ぶことができる世の中へ。

旺文社

大学入試 全レベル問題集

英語長文

駿台予備学校講師 三浦淳一 著

6 国公立大レベル

三訂版

はじめに

　大学受験に向けた英語学習は，書店の学習参考書コーナーに行けばすぐにわかるとおり，とても細分化されています。単語・熟語，文法・語法，構文，英作文，長文読解，リスニング，会話表現，発音・アクセント…

　これを1つずつやっていたら，何年かかっても終わりそうにありません。

　「一石二鳥」という言葉がありますが，短期間で英語の学習を仕上げるには，いわば「一石五鳥」「一石六鳥」の学習をすることです。つまり，1つの学習で複数の効果を得られるような学習をすべきなのです。

　『大学入試 全レベル問題集 英語長文』シリーズは，長文読解の問題集という形をとっていますが，これにとどまらず，語彙力をつけたり，重要な文法事項の確認をしたり，音声を用いた学習により，発音・アクセント，リスニングの力をつけることも目指しています。

　本シリーズはレベル別に6段階で構成されており，必ず自分にピッタリ合った1冊があるはずです。また，現時点の実力と志望校のレベルにギャップがあるなら，1〜2段階レベルを下げて，英語力を基礎から鍛え直すのもおすすめです。受験生はもちろん，高校1・2年生からスタートすることもできます。

　本シリーズは最新の大学入試問題の傾向に対応し，さらに，英語4技能（Reading / Listening / Writing / Speaking）を今後ますます重視する入試制度にも対応しうる，本質的・普遍的な英語力をつけることを目的にしています。

　本シリーズを利用して，皆さんが第一志望の大学に合格することはもちろん，その先，一生の武器となる確固たる英語力を身につけてほしいと願っています。

三浦　淳一

目　次

音声について

本書の英文を読み上げた音声を，専用ウェブサイト・スマートフォンアプリで聞くことができます。英文ごとに，全文通し読みの音声（通し聞き）と冒頭の数段落をややゆっくり読んだ音声（ディクテーション用）の2種類の音声を収録しています。🔊 01のように示しています。

●ウェブサイトで聞く方法

・以下のサイトにアクセスし，パスワードを入力してください。

　https://service.obunsha.co.jp/tokuten/zlr3/

　※すべて半角英数字。検索エンジンの「検索欄」は不可。

　パスワード：zlr3s

●スマートフォンアプリで聞く方法

・音声をスマートフォンアプリ「英語の友」で聞くことができます。「英語の友」で検索するか，右の二次元コードからアクセスしてください。

・パスワードを求められたら，上と同じパスワードを入力してください。

△ご注意ください　◆音声を再生する際の通信料にご注意ください。◆音声は MP3 形式となっています。音声の再生には MP3 を再生できる機器などが別途必要です。デジタルオーディオプレーヤーなどの機器への音声ファイルの転送方法は，各製品の取り扱い説明書などをご覧ください。ご使用機器，音声再生ソフトなどに関する技術的なご質問は，ハードメーカーもしくはソフトメーカーにお問い合わせください。◆スマートフォンやタブレットでは音声をダウンロードできないことがあります。◆本サービスは予告なく終了することがあります。

本シリーズと本書（レベル６）の特長

「大学入試 全レベル問題集 英語長文」シリーズには，以下の特長があります。

1. **細かく分かれたレベル設定**
   本シリーズはレベル別からなる６冊で構成されており，学習者の皆さんそれぞれがベストな１冊を選んで大学入試対策をスタートできるようにしています。各書がレベルに応じた収録英文数と設問構成になっています。

2. **語彙力を重視**
   語彙力は語学学習における基本です。単語がわからなければ英文を読むにも書くにも不自由します。本書ではオールラウンドな語彙力をつけられるよう，幅広いテーマの英文を選びました。各ユニットの最後に，本文の単熟語や英文が復習できる確認問題や，音声を利用した単語のディクテーション問題を設け，語彙力を増強できるよう工夫しています。

3. **全体像をつかむ**
   本書（レベル６）は難度の高い長文の入試問題を中心に収録しています。段落ごとの役割を整理した「パラグラフ展開」を参考に，全体像を把握しながら読む習慣をつけましょう。また，「テーマ解説」は，英文を読む際の背景知識として参考にしてください。

4. **設問の的確な解説**
   すべての設問に，できるだけ短く端的な解説をつけました。また本文の内容に関する設問には，解答の根拠となる箇所を明示して解説しており，類書と比較しても，わかりやすく論理的な解説になっています。これは，解説を読んでわずかな疑問も残してほしくない，さらにはそれ以上に，読者の皆さんが問題を解くときにも，このように論理的に考えて，正解を導き出せるようになってほしいからです。

5. **英文理解の補助**
   複雑な構造の英文には，英文理解の補助として，ＳＶＯＣ分析を付しました。また，本文の和訳例はあまり意訳をせず，文構造を反映させた直訳に近い日本語になっています。

6. **音声による学習**
   付属の音声には，本書に掲載した**英文の音声が２パターン**で収録されています。まず，ナチュラルスピードで全文を通して聞き，シャドーイング*1やオーバーラッピング*2を行ってリスニング力を向上させましょう。次に，冒頭の数段落をゆっくり読んだ音声でディクテーション問題に挑戦しましょう。

   > ＊1　シャドーイング・・・すぐ後から音声を追いかけて，同じ内容を口に出す練習方法
   > ＊2　オーバーラッピング・・・流れてくる音声とぴったり重なるように口に出す練習方法

著者紹介：**三浦淳一**（みうら じゅんいち）

早稲田大学文学部卒。現在，駿台予備学校・医学部受験専門予備校 YMS 講師。『全国大学入試問題正解 英語』（旺文社）解答・解説執筆者。『入門 英語長文問題精講［3 訂版］』『医学部の英語』『大学入学共通テスト 英語［リーディング］集中講座』（以上，旺文社），『世界一覚えやすい中学英語の基本文例 100』（以上，KADOKAWA）ほか著書多数。「Ｎ予備校」「学びエイド」などで映像授業も担当する。

〔協力各氏・各社〕

装丁デザイン：ライトパブリシティ　　　　録 音・編 集：ユニバ合同会社
本文デザイン：イイタカデザイン　　　　　ナレーション：Ann Slater, Guy Perryman, Katie Adler
校　　　　正：白石あゆみ，武田裕之　　　編 集 協 力：株式会社カルチャー・プロ
　　　　　　　　　　　　　　　　　　　　編 集 担 当：嶋田諭示

志望校レベルと「全レベル問題集 英語長文」シリーズのレベル対応表

＊ 掲載の大学名は本シリーズを購入していただく際の目安です。また，大学名は刊行時のものです。

本書のレベル	各レベルの該当大学
① 基礎レベル	高校基礎〜大学受験準備
② 共通テストレベル	共通テストレベル
③ 私大標準レベル	日本大学・東洋大学・駒澤大学・専修大学・京都産業大学・近畿大学・甲南大学・龍谷大学・札幌大学・亜細亜大学・國學院大學・東京電機大学・武蔵大学・神奈川大学・愛知大学・東海大学・名城大学・追手門学院大学・神戸学院大学・広島国際大学・松山大学・福岡大学 他
④ 私大上位レベル	学習院大学・明治大学・青山学院大学・立教大学・中央大学・法政大学・芝浦工業大学・成城大学・成蹊大学・津田塾大学・東京理科大学・日本女子大学・明治学院大学・獨協大学・北里大学・南山大学・関西外国語大学・西南学院大学 他
⑤ 私大最難関レベル	早稲田大学・慶應義塾大学・上智大学・関西大学・関西学院大学・同志社大学・立命館大学 他
⑥ 国公立大レベル	北海道大学・東北大学・東京大学・一橋大学・東京工業大学・名古屋大学・京都大学・大阪大学・神戸大学・広島大学・九州大学 他

本書で使用している記号一覧

🔊 ⋯⋯⋯⋯⋯⋯ 音声番号

文構造 Check!

S, V, O, C ⋯⋯⋯ 主節における文の要素

S, V, O, C ⋯⋯⋯ 従属節における文の要素

S′, V′, O′, C′ ⋯⋯ 意味上の関係

① ② ③ ⋯⋯⋯⋯ 並列関係にある要素

〈　　〉⋯⋯⋯⋯ 名詞句，名詞節

〔　　〕⋯⋯⋯⋯ 形容詞句，形容詞節

（　　）⋯⋯⋯⋯ 副詞句，副詞節

関代 ⋯⋯⋯⋯⋯⋯ 関係代名詞

関副 ⋯⋯⋯⋯⋯⋯ 関係副詞

関形 ⋯⋯⋯⋯⋯⋯ 関係形容詞

等接 ⋯⋯⋯⋯⋯⋯ 等位接続詞

従接 ⋯⋯⋯⋯⋯⋯ 従属接続詞

疑 ⋯⋯⋯⋯⋯⋯⋯ 疑問詞

… so 〜 that … 相関語句

語句リスト

動 ⋯⋯⋯⋯⋯⋯ 動詞

名 ⋯⋯⋯⋯⋯⋯ 名詞

形 ⋯⋯⋯⋯⋯⋯ 形容詞

副 ⋯⋯⋯⋯⋯⋯ 副詞

接 ⋯⋯⋯⋯⋯⋯ 接続詞

前 ⋯⋯⋯⋯⋯⋯ 前置詞

熟 ⋯⋯⋯⋯⋯⋯ 熟語

志望大学別 入試長文分析と学習アドバイス

大学名	北海道大学	東北大学	筑波大学
英文レベル*	 ★3.0　1……2……3……4	3.1★　1……2……3……4	3.0★　1……2……3……4
出題ジャンル	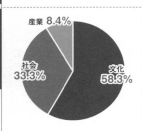 産業 8.4% 社会 33.3% 文化 58.3%	 科学・技術 10.0% 自然 10.0% 社会 10.0% 日常生活 10.0% 文化 60.0%	 自然 16.7% 文化 33.2% 科学・技術 16.7% 社会 16.7% 日常生活 16.7%
	長文問題の平均出題大問数 **4.0 題**	長文問題の平均出題大問数 **3.0 題**	長文問題の平均出題大問数 **2.0 題**
	長文1題あたり平均語数 **796 語**	長文1題あたり平均語数 **828 語**	長文1題あたり平均語数 **785 語**
設問形式	☑内容一致（選択式） ☐内容一致（T or F） ☑空所補充 ☑下線部言い換え ☐表題選択 ☑下線部和訳 ☑記述説明 ☑その他	☑内容一致（選択式） ☐内容一致（T or F） ☑空所補充 ☑下線部言い換え ☐表題選択 ☑下線部和訳 ☑記述説明 ☑その他	☑内容一致（選択式） ☐内容一致（T or F） ☑空所補充 ☑下線部言い換え ☐表題選択 ☐下線部和訳 ☑記述説明 ☑その他
三浦先生Check!	国公立大には珍しく空所補充や内容一致問題が出題される。内容一致問題の選択肢は本文の記述と順序が一致しない。	論説文2題＋会話文（ディスカッション）1題。和訳・説明問題が中心。説明問題は字数制限がなく，本文の深い理解が要求される。	700〜800語前後の長文2題。設問は記述説明問題が中心だが，実質的に和訳を求める問題も含まれる。

※T or F：内容真偽判定問題

6

千葉大学	東京大学	東京医科歯科大学

千葉大学

3.1 ⭐
1 ⋯⋯⋯ 2 ⋯⋯⋯ 3 ⋯⋯⋯ 4

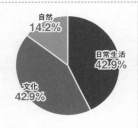

自然 14.2%
日常生活 42.9%
文化 42.9%

長文問題の平均出題大問数
2.3 題

長文1題あたり平均語数
909 語

- ☑ 内容一致（選択式）
- ☑ 内容一致（T or F）
- ☑ 空所補充
- ☑ 下線部言い換え
- ☐ 表題選択
- ☑ 下線部和訳
- ☑ 記述説明
- ☑ その他

800 語前後の論説文2題が基本。和訳・説明のほか，内容一致なども。設問数が多いが，設問ごとの記述量は多くない（字数制限なし）。

東京大学

3.5 ⭐
1 ⋯⋯⋯ 2 ⋯⋯⋯ 3 ⋯⋯⋯ 4

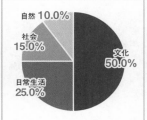

自然 10.0%
社会 15.0%
文化 50.0%
日常生活 25.0%

長文問題の平均出題大問数
3.0 題

長文1題あたり平均語数
593 語

- ☑ 内容一致（選択式）
- ☐ 内容一致（T or F）
- ☑ 空所補充
- ☐ 下線部言い換え
- ☐ 表題選択
- ☑ 下線部和訳
- ☑ 記述説明
- ☑ その他

要約・下線部和訳・語句整序・空所補充問題など多様な出題形式。エッセイや小説も出る。設問が多いので時間配分に注意する必要がある。

東京医科歯科大学

3.4 ⭐
1 ⋯⋯⋯ 2 ⋯⋯⋯ 3 ⋯⋯⋯ 4

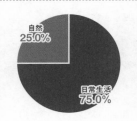

自然 25.0%
日常生活 75.0%

長文問題の平均出題大問数
1.0 題

長文1題あたり平均語数
1,783 語

- ☐ 内容一致（選択式）
- ☑ 内容一致（T or F）
- ☐ 空所補充
- ☑ 下線部言い換え
- ☐ 表題選択
- ☑ 下線部和訳
- ☑ 記述説明
- ☑ その他

同一の英文を全学科で共有しつつ，設問は学科ごとに異なる。共通問題の内容真偽は 20 以上の選択肢があり，本文の正確な理解が求められる。

大学名	東京外国語大学	東京工業大学	一橋大学
英文レベル※	3.7 ★ 1……2……3……4	3.4 ★ 1……2……3……4	3.8 ★ 1……2……3……4
出題ジャンル	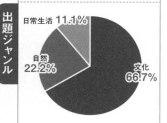 日常生活 11.1% 自然 22.2% 文化 66.7%	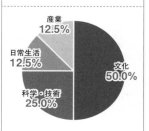 産業 12.5% 日常生活 12.5% 科学・技術 25.0% 文化 50.0%	社会 44.4% 文化 55.6%
	長文問題の平均出題大問数 **2.0 題**	長文問題の平均出題大問数 **2.0 題**	長文問題の平均出題大問数 **1.0 題**
	長文1題あたり平均語数 **886 語**	長文1題あたり平均語数 **1,630 語**	長文1題あたり平均語数 **1,406 語**
設問形式	☐ 内容一致（選択式） ☐ 内容一致（T or F） ☑ 空所補充 ☐ 下線部言い換え ☐ 表題選択 ☐ 下線部和訳 ☑ 記述説明 ☐ その他	☑ 内容一致（選択式） ☐ 内容一致（T or F） ☑ 空所補充 ☑ 下線部言い換え ☐ 表題選択 ☑ 下線部和訳 ☑ 記述説明 ☑ その他	☑ 内容一致（選択式） ☐ 内容一致（T or F） ☑ 空所補充 ☐ 下線部言い換え ☐ 表題選択 ☑ 下線部和訳 ☑ 記述説明 ☐ その他
三浦先生Check!	長文2題で総語数は約2,000語にもなる。大問1は記述量が非常に多い。大問2は語形変化を含む空所補充問題のみ。	長文2題。うち1題は2,000語前後と非常に長い。和訳・説明問題のほか，内容一致問題も出題される。英作文が含まれるのが特徴的。	説明・和訳問題のほか，空所補充問題も出題される。英文は難度が高く，高度な語彙力が求められる。社会科学系のテーマが多い。

※T or F：内容真偽判定問題

横浜国立大学

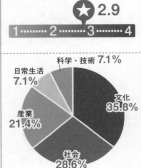

★2.9

1┄┄┄2┄┄┄3┄┄┄4

科学・技術 7.1%
日常生活 7.1%
産業 21.4%
社会 28.6%
文化 35.8%

長文問題の平均出題大問数
2.3 題

長文1題あたり平均語数
577 語

- ☐ 内容一致（選択式）
- ☐ 内容一致（T or F）
- ☑ 空所補充
- ☐ 下線部言い換え
- ☐ 表題選択
- ☑ 下線部和訳
- ☑ 記述説明
- ☑ その他

2題で合計800語前後。現代的なテーマが多い。"Explain the content of…" のように英語で指示される設問は実質的に和訳問題。

新潟大学

★2.6

1┄┄┄2┄┄┄3┄┄┄4

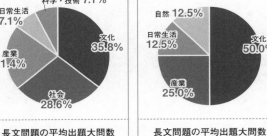

自然 12.5%
日常生活 12.5%
産業 25.0%
文化 50.0%

長文問題の平均出題大問数
2.0 題

長文1題あたり平均語数
535 語

- ☐ 内容一致（選択式）
- ☐ 内容一致（T or F）
- ☐ 空所補充
- ☐ 下線部言い換え
- ☐ 表題選択
- ☑ 下線部和訳
- ☑ 記述説明
- ☐ その他

500 ～ 600 語前後の論説文2題が基本。出題形式は和訳・説明問題のみ。和訳問題は易しめだが，説明問題の記述量が多い。

名古屋大学

3.4★

1┄┄┄2┄┄┄3┄┄┄4

自然 8.3%
科学・技術 16.7%
日常生活 41.7%
文化 33.3%

長文問題の平均出題大問数
3.0 題

長文1題あたり平均語数
664 語

- ☑ 内容一致（選択式）
- ☐ 内容一致（T or F）
- ☑ 空所補充
- ☑ 下線部言い換え
- ☐ 表題選択
- ☑ 下線部和訳
- ☑ 記述説明
- ☑ その他

論説文2題＋会話文1題が基本。難易度が年度により上下する。和訳・説明問題を中心に，文補充や語句整序も出題される。

大学名	京都大学	大阪大学	神戸大学
英文レベル※	4.0 ★ 1……2……3……4	3.7 ★ 1……2……3……4	★ 2.9 1……2……3……4
出題ジャンル	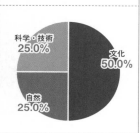 科学・技術 25.0% / 文化 50.0% / 自然 25.0%	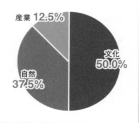 産業 12.5% / 文化 50.0% / 自然 37.5%	 科学・技術 8.4% / 文化 33.3% / 日常生活 25.0% / 自然 33.3%

長文問題の平均出題大問数 **2.0 題** / 長文1題あたり平均語数 **605 語**（京都大学）

長文問題の平均出題大問数 **2.0 題** / 長文1題あたり平均語数 **988 語**（大阪大学）

長文問題の平均出題大問数 **3.0 題** / 長文1題あたり平均語数 **606 語**（神戸大学）

設問形式

設問形式	京都大学	大阪大学	神戸大学
内容一致（選択式）	☐	☑	☑
内容一致（T or F）	☐	☐	☐
空所補充	☐	☐	☑
下線部言い換え	☐	☑	☑
表題選択	☐	☐	☐
下線部和訳	☑	☑	☑
記述説明	☑	☑	☑
その他	☐	☑	☑

三浦先生Check!

京都大学：抽象度の高い，難解な英文が中心。以前は下線部和訳問題のみだったが，近年は説明問題等も出題されるようになった。

大阪大学：大問1は短めの英文で下線部または全文和訳問題。大問2が長文総合問題（外国語学部は別）。難易度は年度にもよるが概して高い。

神戸大学：500語前後の論説文2題と小説が1題。出題形式は和訳・説明・内容一致問題。説明問題の字数制限がやや厳しい年度もある。

※T or F：内容真偽判定問題

岡山大学

★3.0
1……2……3……4

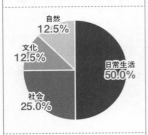

自然 12.5%
文化 12.5%
日常生活 50.0%
社会 25.0%

長文問題の平均出題大問数
2.0 題

長文1題あたり平均語数
922 語

- ☑ 内容一致（選択式）
- ☐ 内容一致（T or F）
- ☑ 空所補充
- ☑ 下線部言い換え
- ☐ 表題選択
- ☐ 下線部和訳
- ☑ 記述説明
- ☑ その他

論説文1題に加えエッセイなど1題で総語数は2,000語近い。説明問題は字数制限がないが、過不足なく丁寧に記述することが求められる。

九州大学

★2.8
1……2……3……4

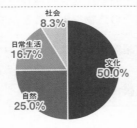

社会 8.3%
日常生活 16.7%
文化 50.0%
自然 25.0%

長文問題の平均出題大問数
3.0 題

長文1題あたり平均語数
556 語

- ☑ 内容一致（選択式）
- ☐ 内容一致（T or F）
- ☑ 空所補充
- ☑ 下線部言い換え
- ☑ 表題選択
- ☑ 下線部和訳
- ☑ 記述説明
- ☑ その他

500～600語前後の長文が3題。和訳、説明、内容一致問題が中心。説明問題は書くべき内容を細かく指定される場合があり、記述量は概して多め。

熊本大学

★2.8
1……2……3……4

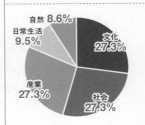

自然 8.6%
日常生活 9.5%
文化 27.3%
産業 27.3%
社会 27.3%

長文問題の平均出題大問数
2.8 題

長文1題あたり平均語数
950 語

- ☑ 内容一致（選択式）
- ☐ 内容一致（T or F）
- ☑ 空所補充
- ☑ 下線部言い換え
- ☐ 表題選択
- ☑ 下線部和訳
- ☑ 記述説明
- ☑ その他

500～600語程度の論説文（またはエッセイ）2題と会話文。論説文のうち1題は日本語での記述（和訳・説明）、1題は英問英答式。

掲載データは、『2021年受験用 全国大学入試問題正解 英語』～『2024年受験用 全国大学入試問題正解 英語』を旺文社編集部が独自に分析したものです。

解答

問

(1) 彼は，ナバホ語を話しているのを見つけられたときに，口をゆすぐために教師に強制的に使わせられた，まずい茶色の石けんの味を口の中に再現できそうなほどであった。

(2) いかなる状況下のいかなる時においても，彼らは許可なく，あるいは1人でその建物を出ることができなかった。

(3) 彼ら自身の言語を話したことを理由にかつて彼らを罰したことのある政府が今，戦争に勝つ助けとなるために彼らにその言語を使うように頼んできていたのだ。

解説

問

(1)

He could almost taste the harsh brown soap the teachers had forced him to use to wash his mouth out when he was caught speaking Navajo.

> **訳** 彼は，ナバホ語を話しているのを見つけられたときに，口をゆすぐために教師に強制的に使わせられた，まずい茶色の石けんの味を口の中に再現できそうなほどであった。

以下のポイントをおさえよう！

- ☑ could almost taste の部分は，直訳すれば「ほとんど味わうことができた」。ここでは，子供のころに経験した味を舌が覚えていることを表現しているので，「味がしそうなほどであった」，「味を再現できそうなほどであった」などと工夫して訳出する。
- ☑ harsh は「厳しい，過酷な」の意味が一般的だが，「**(味・音・色などが)不快な，きつすぎる**」の意味もある。
- ☑ soap の後に**目的格の関係代名詞 which [that] が省略**されている。
- ☑ ⟨**force ＋ O ＋ to** *do*⟩「**O に～するよう強制する**」
- ☑ to wash ... は**不定詞の副詞用法**で【**目的**】を表す。

☑ **wash *one*'s mouth out**「口をゆすぐ」。なお，会話表現で "Wash your mouth out with soap." は，直訳すれば「石けんで口をゆすぎなさい」だが，下品な言葉などを使った相手をたしなめる言い方。

☑ 〈**catch＋O＋*doing***〉「O が～しているのを見つける」

(2)

At no time under any circumstances were they to leave the building without permission or alone.

> 訳 いかなる状況下のいかなる時においても，彼らは許可なく，あるいは１人でその建物を出ることができなかった。

以下のポイントをおさえよう！

☑ At no time under any circumstances「いかなる状況のいかなる時にも…ない」は否定の副詞句であり，**文頭に否定の副詞があると主語と動詞は倒置され**疑問文の語順になる。

☑ were they to … の部分は，be to *do* の形になっている。**be to *do*** は【義務】【予定】【運命】【可能】【意図】などの意味を表すが，ここでは【義務】（否定文なので【禁止】）を表すと考える。

☑ without permission と alone が **or により並列**されている。

(3)

Now this government that had punished them in the past for speaking their own language was asking them to use it to help win the war.

> 訳 彼ら自身の言語を話したことを理由にかつて彼らを罰したことのある政府が今，戦争に勝つ助けとなるために彼らにその言語を使うように頼んできていたのだ。

以下のポイントをおさえよう！

☑ that は主格の関係代名詞で，節の範囲は language まで。

☑ **punish *A* for *B***「B(こと)により A(人)を罰する」

☑ 〈**ask＋O＋to *do***〉「O に～するよう頼む」

☑ to help … は**不定詞の副詞用法で【目的】**を表し，use を修飾。

☑ help win … の部分は，**help to *do***「～するのを助ける，～するのに役立つ」

の **to** が省略されている。

▼

それでは次に，段落ごとに詳しく見ていこう。

第1段落

¹Eugene Crawford is a Navajo, a Native American; he cannot forget the day he and his friends were recruited for the United States military. **²Upon arrival at Camp Elliott, they were led to a**
→p.15 文構造Check!
classroom, which reminded him of the ones he had entered in boarding schools as a child. ³Those memories were far from pleasant. **⁴He could almost taste the harsh brown soap the**
→p.15 文構造Check!
teachers had forced him to use to wash his mouth out when he was caught speaking Navajo. ⁵His thoughts were interrupted when the door suddenly opened and an officer entered. ⁶The new recruits stood to attention. "⁷At ease, gentlemen. ⁸Please be seated."

訳 ¹ユージン・クローフォードはナバホ族，つまり先住アメリカ人である。彼は自分と友人がアメリカ軍に入隊した日のことを忘れることができない。²エリオットキャンプに到着次第，彼らは教室に連れて行かれた。その教室は彼に，子供のころ全寮制学校で入っていった教室を思い出させた。³その記憶は決して楽しいものではなかった。⁴彼は，ナバホ語を話しているのを見つけられたときに，口をゆすぐために教師に強制的に使わせられた，まずい茶色の石けんの味を口の中に再現できそうなほどであった。⁵ドアが突然開き，士官が入ってきて，彼の思考は中断させられた。⁶新入隊員たちは気をつけの姿勢をした。「⁷休め，諸君。⁸着席」。

語 句

recruit	動	新規に採用する，入隊させる／
	名	新入社員，新入隊員
military	名	軍隊
upon[on] (*one's*) arrival	熟	到着次第，到着時に
remind *A* of *B*	熟	A に B を思い出させる
boarding school	名	全寮制学校

memory	名	記憶，思い出
far from ~	熟	決して～ではない
pleasant	形	楽しい，気持ちのよい
taste	動	味わう，味を感じる
harsh	形	不快な
force	動	強制する
▶ **force**＋**O**＋**to** *do*		O に～するよう強制する

14

wash out	熟 きれいに洗う，(容器などの) 中まで洗う	interrupt	動 中断させる，さえぎる
catch	動 見つける	stand to attention	熟 気をつけをする， 気をつけの姿勢で立つ
▶ **catch**+**O**+***doing***	O が～しているのを 見つける	at ease	熟 気楽に，《号令》休め
thought	名 思考，考え	be seated	熟 座る

文構造Check!

(Upon arrival 〔 at Camp Elliott 〕),

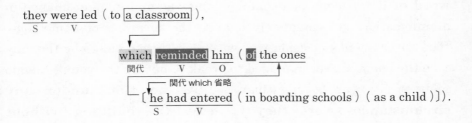

▶ which は関係代名詞の非制限用法で，a classroom を指す。the ones は the classrooms の代用。*ones* の後に目的格の関係代名詞 which[that] の省略。

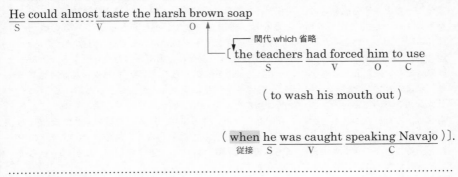

▶ 設問の解説(p.12)参照。

¹The first hour they spent in that building changed their lives forever, and the shock of what occurred is still felt by them to this day. ²They could never have imagined the project the military had recruited them for. ³**Some of them believed that, had they known beforehand, they might not have joined up so eagerly.**
→ p.17 文構造Check!

⁴**Navajo had been chosen as a code for secret messages**
→ p.17 文構造Check!
because unless you were a Navajo, you'd never understand a word of it. ⁵Navajo is a complex language and a slight change in pronunciation can completely change the meaning of a message. ⁶The government's decision was wise — it turned out to be the only code the enemy never managed to break — but for the young Navajo soldiers, it was a nightmare. ⁷**At no time under any circumstances were they to leave the building without**
→ p.17 文構造Check!
permission or alone. ⁸They were forbidden to tell anyone about the project, even their families, until it was finally made public in 1968.

訳 ¹その建物で過ごした最初の1時間が，彼らの人生を永久に変えるものとなった。そこで起こった出来事の衝撃を今日でもなお，彼らは感じ取っている。²彼らは軍隊が自分たちを入隊させた目的となる計画のことなど，想像だにしなかったであろう。³一部の者たちは，事前に知っていたら，それほど熱心な気持ちで入隊しなかったかもしれないと思った。⁴ナバホ語は秘密のメッセージのための暗号として選ばれたのであった。なぜなら，ナバホ族の者でない限り，だれもそれを一言も理解できないからだ。⁵ナバホ語は複雑な言語であり，発音のわずかな違いがメッセージの意味を完全に変えてしまうこともある。⁶政府の決断は賢明なものであった。ナバホ語は敵がどうやっても破れない唯一の暗号であることが判明したのだ。だが，若きナバホ族の兵士たちにとっては，それは悪夢のような経験であった。⁷いかなる状況下のいかなる時においても，彼らは許可なく，あるいは1人でその建物を出ることができなかった。⁸彼らはその計画について，1968年についに公にされるまで，だれにも，家族にさえも話すことを禁じられていたのだ。

語 句

forever	副	永久に
imagine	動	想像する
project	名	計画，企画
beforehand	副	前もって，事前に
join up	熟	入隊する
eagerly	副	熱心に
code	名	暗号
slight	形	わずかな，少しの
pronunciation	名	発音
completely	副	完全に
government	名	政府
turn out to be ～	熟	結局～だとわかる
enemy	名	敵
manage to *do*	熟	どうにか～する
soldier	名	兵士
nightmare	名	悪夢(のような経験)
circumstance	名	状況
permission	名	許可
forbid	動	禁ずる

▶ **forbid + O + to *do*** Oが～するのを禁ずる

文構造Check!

Some of them believed 〈 that, (had they known beforehand),
S   V   O従接   S   V

they might not have joined up (so eagerly)〉.
S   V

▶ had they known beforehand は if they had known beforehand (had known＝仮定法過去完了) の if が省略され，主語と助動詞が倒置された形。

Navajo had been chosen (as a code 〔 for secret messages 〕)
S   V

(because (unless you were a Navajo),
従接   従接   S   V   C

you'd never understand a word of it).
S   V   O

▶ because が導く副詞節の中に unless が導く副詞節が入っている。

(At no time) (under any circumstances)

were they to leave the building (without permission or alone).
S   V   O   ①   等接 ②

▶ 設問の解説(p.13)参照。

17

第3段落

¹**Many of these men had been punished, sometimes brutally,**
→文構造Check!
for speaking Navajo in classrooms similar to this, classrooms
in schools run by the same government. ²**Now this**
→ p.19 文構造Check!
government that had punished them in the past for speaking
their own language was asking them to use it to help win the
war. ³White people were stranger than the Navajo had imagined.

> **訳** ¹この男たちの多くは，今回の教室と似たような教室で，つまり，同じ政府によって運営されている学校の教室で，ナバホ語を話したことにより，時には厳しく罰せられた経験を持っていた。²彼ら自身の言語を話したことを理由にかつて彼らを罰したことのある政府が今，戦争に勝つ助けとなるために彼らにその言語を使うように頼んできていたのだ。³白人はナバホ族が想像した以上に奇妙な人々であった。

語句

punish 動 罰する	**(be) similar to ~** 熟 ~に似て
▶ **punish A for B** A(人)をB(事)により罰する	**run** 動 運営する，営む
	＊活用：run-ran-run
brutally 副 容赦なく，残忍に	**past** 名 過去
	▶ **in the past** 過去に，かつて

文構造Check!

Many of these men had been punished, (sometimes brutally),
　　　　S　　　　　　　　　V

　　　　　　(for speaking Navajo)

(in classrooms 〔 similar to this 〕, classrooms 〔 in schools 〔 run by the same
　　　　　　　　└───同格───┘

government 〕〕).

....

▶ punish A for B「AをBにより罰する」が受動態になっている。

classrooms similar to this と classrooms ... government が同格。

18

Now this government
　　　　　　S

[that had punished them (in the past) (for speaking their own language)]
関代　　V　　　　　O

was asking them to use it (to help win the war).
　　　V　　　O　　　　　　　　C　　　　　　　　(to)

▶ 設問の解説(p.13)参照。

第1段落

ナバホ族であるユージン・クローフォードの回想

　アメリカ軍に登用され，エリオットキャンプに来たユージン・クローフォードは教室に入る

　子供時代の不愉快な経験(ナバホ語を話すことが禁じられた)が思い出される

第2段落

ナバホ族がアメリカ軍に登用された理由

　ナバホ語は複雑で難解な言語

　アメリカ政府は暗号としてナバホ語を使うことを決定

　ナバホ族の者にとっては，行動が制約され，悪夢のようだった

第3段落

アメリカ政府の豹変する態度

　かつてはナバホ語を話す者を，学校教育の場で厳しく罰していた

　今や戦争に勝つためにナバホ語を使うように要請してきている

テーマ解説

　言語に関する英文は入試問題頻出であり，消滅の危機に瀕している少数民族の言語についても頻出テーマとなる。本英文は少々変わった切り口で，いわゆるコードトーカー(傍受される可能性の高い無線交信に暗号として解読困難な部族語を用いるため，アメリカ軍に登用された先住民族)の観点から書かれた英文である。

確認問題

/40点

1. ①〜⑩は語句の意味を日本語で書き，⑪〜⑳は和訳と対応する英語の語句を，頭文字を参考にして書き，空欄を完成させよう。（各1点×20）

① military 　名 　

② pleasant 　形 　

③ interrupt 　動 　

④ beforehand 　副 　

⑤ eagerly 　副 　

⑥ code 　名 　

⑦ pronunciation 　名 　

⑧ completely 　副 　

⑨ nightmare 　名 　

⑩ forbid + O + to *do* 　熟 　O が〜するのを

⑪ upon [on] (*one's*) a　 　熟 　到着次第，到着時に

⑫ m 　名 　記憶，思い出

⑬ f + O + to *do* 　熟 　O に〜するよう強制する

⑭ c + O + *doing* 　熟 　O が〜しているのを見つける

⑮ f 　副 　永久に

⑯ i 　動 　想像する

⑰ pr 　名 　計画，企画

⑱ s 　形 　わずかな，少しの

⑲ t o to be 〜 　熟 　結局〜だとわかる

⑳ e 　名 　敵

2. 次の[　]の語句を並べ替えて，意味の通る英文を完成させよう。（各5点×2）

① They were led to a classroom, [which / the ones / entered / him / of / reminded / he / had] in boarding schools as a child.

彼らは教室に連れて行かれた。その教室は彼に，子供のころ全寮制学校で入っていた教室を思い出させた。

② At no time [circumstances / they / leave / to / the building / under / any / were] without permission or alone.

いかなる状況下のいかなる時においても，彼らは許可なく，あるいは1人でその建物を出ることができなかった。

---

3. 次の英文を和訳してみよう。(10 点)

Now this government that had punished them in the past for speaking their own language was asking them to use it to help win the war.

ディクテーションしてみよう！

今回学習した英文に出てきた語句を，音声を聞いて＿＿＿＿に書き取ろう。

04   Eugene Crawford is a Navajo, a Native American; he cannot forget the day he and his friends were recruited for the United States military. ❶＿＿＿＿＿＿ Camp Elliott, they were led to a classroom, which reminded him of the ones he had entered in boarding schools as a child. Those memories ❷＿＿＿＿＿＿＿＿＿. He could almost taste the harsh brown soap the teachers had forced him to use to wash his mouth out ❸＿＿＿＿＿＿＿＿＿＿ Navajo. His thoughts were interrupted when the door suddenly opened and an officer entered. The new recruits stood to attention. "At ease, gentlemen. Please be seated."

05   ❹＿＿＿＿＿＿＿＿＿＿＿＿＿＿ changed their lives forever, and the shock of what occurred is still felt by them to this day. They could never have imagined the project the military had recruited them for. Some of them believed that, ❺＿＿＿＿＿＿＿＿＿, they might not have joined up so eagerly. Navajo had been chosen as a code for secret messages because unless you were a Navajo, you'd never understand a word of it. Navajo is a complex language and a slight change in pronunciation

can ❻_____. The government's
decision was wise — it turned out to be the only code the enemy never
managed to break — but for the young Navajo soldiers, it was a nightmare.
At no time under any circumstances were they to leave the building without
permission or alone. They were ❼_____,
even their families, until it was finally made public in 1968.

確認問題の答

1. ①軍隊 　②楽しい，気持ちのよい 　③中断させる，さえぎる 　④前もって，事前に
   ⑤熱心に 　⑥暗号 　⑦発音 　⑧完全に 　⑨悪夢(のような経験) 　⑩禁ずる 　⑪arrival
   ⑫memory 　⑬force 　⑭catch 　⑮forever 　⑯imagine 　⑰project 　⑱slight
   ⑲turn out 　⑳enemy

2. ① which reminded him of the ones he had entered 　（第1段落　第2文）
   ② under any circumstances were they to leave the building 　（第2段落　第7文）

3. 彼ら自身の言語を話したことを理由にかつて彼らを罰したことのある政府が今，戦争に勝つ助けとなるため
   に彼らにその言語を使うように頼んできていたのだ。　（第3段落　第2文）

ディクテーションしてみよう！の答

❶ Upon arrival at 　❷ were far from pleasant
❸ when he was caught speaking 　❹ The first hour they spent in that building
❺ had they known beforehand 　❻ completely change the meaning of a message
❼ forbidden to tell anyone about the project

2 解答・解説

解答

問1 クラウドや外部ドライブ，タブレット，スマートフォンなどのデータ保存装置が常に変化しており，重大な変化が生じるたびに，データが失われる可能性が常にあるということ。

問2 例えば，大規模な太陽フレアがアマゾン，アップル，フェイスブックその他のデータセンターを壊滅させた場合や，これらの企業の1つが倒産した場合のように，クラウドに蓄積されたデータが失われ，私たちがデジタル文化を失いうる状況は数多く存在するという難点。

問3 私たちがほとんど考えない文化の小さな断片こそが，過去の文化を研究している考古学者や人類学者にこの上なく重要な手がかりや見識をもたらす

問4 **(A)** survival **(B)** dominate **(C)** impacts **(D)** ensure **(E)** critical

問5 文化とは，私たちが日々の生活と世の中を進んでいくために使う知識である。

解説

問1

(1)The problem with this data storage is that it is changing all the time and with every significant change there is always the possibility of losing data.

　下線部の直後に is that ... と続くので，that 以下を訳せばよい。it は this data storage を指し，this は第1段落第1文の the Cloud and on storage devices like external drives, tablets, and smartphones を受けているので，その内容も含めれば解答としては万全だろう。

　下線部を含む文の構造を確認しよう。

The problem 〔with this data storage〕 is
　　S　　　　　　　　　　　　　　　　　V

〈that it is changing (all the time) and
C　　S　　V

(with every significant change) there is always the possibility of losing data.〉
　　　　　　　　　　　　　　　　　　　V　　　　　　　　　　S

問2

And if you think that (2)keeping it all in the Cloud is the answer, it isn't.

　まず，下線部を含む文で，「そして，全てをクラウドに保管することが解決策であると思っているのなら，それは違う」と述べ，「全てをクラウドに保管すること」に否定的な立場を明らかにしている。根拠となる「難点」はこの後に書かれている。以下のように Or の前後に１つずつ具体例があり，これをまとめる形で The point is that …「要するに…」に続けて「難点」を挙げている。以上をまとめればよい。

具体例①

Take a solar flare as an example. If a major solar flare wipes out Amazon, Apple, Facebook, and other data centers, all will be lost.

具体例②

Or if one of these companies goes bankrupt, it is possible that the data it hosts will be lost.

まとめ

The point is that **there are many ways that we could lose our digital culture**.

問3

This is because (3)it is the small bits and pieces of a culture that we barely think about that often deliver the greatest clues and insights to archeologists and anthropologists studying past cultures.

以下のポイントをおさえよう！

- ☑ it is 〜 that … に注目する。that が2つあるが，1つめの that は直前に名詞があるので関係代名詞と考え，it is は2つめの that とセットになる。2つめの that のあとは S が欠けていることから，強調構文とわかる。「…するのは〜だ」「〜こそ…する」「まさに〜が…する」などと訳す。
- ☑ bits and pieces of 〜 で「〜の断片」。barely は肯定的に「かろうじて〜する」，否定的に「ほとんど〜しない」の意味を持つが，ここでは後者が自然。強調構文で強調される部分(the small 〜 think about)の訳は「私たちがほとんど考えない文化の小さな断片」となる。
- ☑ deliver A to B は「A を B に配達する，引き渡す」が本来の意味だが，ここでは A が抽象的な物なので，「A を B にもたらす」などと意訳する。
- ☑ studying past cultures は現在分詞の形容詞用法で，直前の名詞 archeologists and anthropologists を修飾。

問4

(A) 空欄を含む第3段落第1文には therefore があるので，第2段落の内容からの帰結となるように考える。第2段落では，文化を保存することの重要性を説明している。そこで，a matter of survival「生存の問題，生き残りをかけた問題」とすれば文脈に合う。

(B) come to do で「〜するようになる」。動詞の原形を入れるべきなので，dominate「支配する，優位に立つ」と ensure「確実にする」の二択。空欄の直後に前置詞句が続くので，自動詞を入れるべきであり，ensure は他動詞の用法しかないので不可。

(C) 空欄を含む文の最後に it had on cultures around the world とあるのに注目。have an impact on 〜 で「〜に影響を及ぼす」の意味。ここでは impact が複数形になり，疑問詞 what とセットになって前に移動したと考える。

(D) 空欄が do we の後なので動詞の原形。ensure that … で「…ことを確実にする」の意味。

(E) 空欄が is の後なので，C(補語)となる形容詞を入れる。critical は「重大

26

な」の意味。本文の主題は，文化を保存することの重要性と，それを脅かすクラウドなどの記憶装置の危険性。critical を入れればこの主題にも適合する。

問5

第3段落第4文が Culture is ... 「文化とは…」と始まっているので，この文を訳せばよい。

文構造を確認しよう。

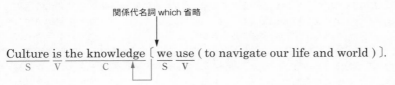

関係代名詞 which 省略

Culture is the knowledge 〔 we use (to navigate our life and world) 〕.
 S   V   C   S V

以下のポイントをおさえよう！

☑ knowledge の後に関係代名詞 which の省略。

☑ to 以下は【目的】を表す不定詞副詞用法。

☑ navigate は「（海などを）航行［航海］する」が本来の意味。比喩的に「（～の中を）進む」の意味を表していると解釈する。

▼

それでは次に，段落ごとに詳しく見ていこう。

06 - 08

第1段落

¹As we put ever more of our lives into the Cloud and on storage devices like external drives, tablets, and smartphones, we place bits and pieces of our culture there as well: music, art, literature, maps, videos, and photos. ²These are all artifacts of our culture. ³The problem with this data storage is that it is changing all the time and with every significant change there is always the possibility of losing data. ⁴And if you think that keeping it all in the Cloud is the

answer, it isn't. ⁵Take a solar flare as an example. ⁶If a major solar flare wipes out Amazon, Apple, Facebook, and other data centers, all will be lost. ⁷Or if one of these companies goes bankrupt, it is possible that the data it hosts will be lost. ⁸The point is that there are many ways that we could lose our digital culture.

訳 ¹私たちがクラウドや外部ドライブ，タブレット，スマートフォンなどのデータ保存装置にますます多くの私たちの生活を入れるにつれて，音楽，芸術，文学，地図，動画，写真など，私たちの文化の断片をもそこに置いている。²これらはすべて私たちの文化の遺物である。³このようなデータ保存の問題点は，それが常に変化しており，重大な変化が生じるたびに，データが失われる可能性が常にあるということだ。⁴そして，全てをクラウドに保管することが解決策であると思っているのなら，それは違う。⁵太陽フレアを例に挙げよう。⁶もし大規模な太陽フレアが Amazon, Apple, Facebook, その他のデータセンターを壊滅させた場合，すべてが失われるだろう。⁷あるいは，これらの企業の１つが倒産した場合，ホストしているデータが失われる可能性がある。⁸要は，私たちのデジタル文化を失いうる状況は数多く存在するということだ。

語句

Cloud	名	クラウド(クラウドコンピューティングの略。インターネット上のデータストレージやサービス)
storage	名	(データなどの)保存，記憶
device	名	装置，器具
external	形	外部の
drive	名	(コンピュータの)ドライブ[駆動装置]
tablet	名	タブレット(タッチスクリーンから操作・入力できる携帯型パソコン)

bits and pieces	熟	小さいもの，細々としたもの
literature	名	文学
artifact	名	(人工)遺物，文化的遺物
significant	形	重要な，重大な
answer	名	正解，解決策
wipe out	熟	全滅[壊滅]させる，根絶する
go bankrupt	熟	倒産する
host	動	ホストする(ウェブサイトなどを提供する)
point	名	要点，大事なこと

▶ **The point is (that) ...** 要するに…

第2段落

¹Such loss of our digital culture could make it difficult for those in the future to understand how we lived. ²This is because it is the small bits and pieces of a culture that we barely think about that often deliver the greatest clues and insights to archeologists and

anthropologists studying past cultures. ³The materials and process used to make an ancient clay pot, for example, tell us about the food culture of the society that made it. ⁴The layout of buildings, to cite another example, can tell us if the society was ruled by a king or queen or if it was more communal. ⁵Studying humanity's past helps us navigate today and seek for the future. ⁶Through archeology and anthropology, we've been able to understand different political systems and methods of governance in the past which have informed how we govern our societies today.

訳 ¹このようなデジタル文化の喪失は，将来の人々が私たちの生活を理解するのを困難にするかもしれない。²これは，私たちがほとんど考えない文化の小さな断片こそが，過去の文化を研究している考古学者や人類学者にこの上なく重要な手がかりや見識をもたらすからだ。³例えば，古代の土器を作るために使用された材料や製法は，それを作った社会の食文化について私たちに教えてくれる。⁴他の例を挙げると，建物の配置は，社会が王や女王によって統治されていたのか，それともより共同社会的だったのかを教えてくれる。⁵人類の過去を研究することは，私たちが今日を生き抜き，未来を探求する上で役立つ。⁶考古学と人類学を通じて，私たちは今日の社会を統治する方法に影響を及ぼしてきた過去のさまざまな政治制度や統治方法を理解することができている。

語句

barely	副 ほとんど〜ない		**layout**	名 レイアウト，配置
deliver	動 届ける，伝える		**cite**	動 (例として)挙げる，引用する
clue	名 手がかり，ヒント		**rule**	動 支配する，統治する
insight	名 洞察，見識		**communal**	形 共同社会の
archeologist	名 考古学者		**humanity**	名 人類
anthropologist	名 人類学者		**navigate**	動 進む，切り抜ける
material	名 材料		**archaeology**	名 考古学
process	名 工程，製法		**anthropology**	名 人類学
clay	名 粘土		**governance**	名 統治
pot	名 鍋，壺，容器		**inform**	動 影響を与える，特徴付ける

第3段落

¹It is therefore a matter of survival that we work to save the artifacts of our digital culture. ²We may in the distant future seek to

understand at what point and how artificial intelligence came to dominate in our societies and how it affected our cultures. ³We may want to know how we let social media run amok and what impacts, good and bad, it had on cultures around the world. ⁴Culture is the knowledge we use to navigate our life and world. ⁵So the question then becomes, how do we ensure that our digital lives and desiderata are preserved as much as possible? ⁶How do they get copied into new storage formats? ⁷Preserving our present for the future is critical for cultural understanding and navigating our world in the future.

> **訳** ¹したがって，私たちのデジタル文化の遺物を保存しようと働くことは，生き残りをかけた問題でもある。²私たちは遠い未来に，人工知能がどの時点でどのようにして私たちの社会で優位に立ったのか，それが私たちの文化にどのような影響を与えたのかを理解しようとしているかもしれない。³私たちはソーシャルメディアをどのように暴走させてしまったのか，それが世界中の文化にどのようなよい影響・悪い影響を与えたのかを知りたいと思うかもしれない。⁴文化とは，私たちが日々の生活と世の中を進んでいくために使う知識である。⁵したがって，問題はどのようにすれば私たちのデジタルな生活と願望ができるだけ保護されるか，ということになる。⁶それらが新しい保存フォーマットにコピーされるようにするにはどうすればよいのか。⁷将来のために私たちの現在を保存することは，文化の理解と将来の世界を生き抜くために重要である。

語句

save	動 保存する，保護する	**preserve**	動 保存する，保護する
artificial intelligence	名 人工知能	format	名 フォーマット（データの保存・読み書きのための形式，書式）
dominate	動 支配する，優位に立つ		
ensure	動 確実にする	**critical**	形 重大な，決定的な
desideratum	名 ぜひ欲しい物 ＊複数形：desiderata		

パラグラフ展開　英文全体の内容を把握しよう！

第1段落 導入

生活や文化をクラウドやデータ保存装置に保存

➡ デジタル文化のデータ喪失のリスク

例 太陽フレア，企業の倒産

第2段落 主張

デジタル文化の喪失

➡ 未来の人々は私たちの生活を理解できない

∵文化の断片 ＝ 過去を知る手がかり

第3段落 結論＆問題提起

デジタル文化の遺物を保存することは重要

➡ デジタル文化を保存するには？

テーマ解説

　本文の主題は「デジタル文化の脆弱性」である。デジタル文化は私たちの生活のあらゆる側面に影響を与えており，便益を提供する一方で，いくつかの脆弱性や問題点もある。本文では，大量のデータが何らかの事故等により失われるリスクが挙げられていた。その他の問題点を見てみよう。

①セキュリティとプライバシーの脅威

　デジタル文化は大量のデータをオンラインで共有する結果，個人情報の漏洩やハッキングなどのセキュリティ上の問題が発生する可能性がある。また，個人のプライバシーがデジタルプラットフォーム上で侵害されることも懸念される。

②デジタルディバイド[digital divide]

　デジタル文化の普及は一部の地域や社会階層に偏っており，デジタルディバイド（テクノロジーの恩恵を受ける者と受けない者との間の情報格差）が拡大している。インターネットを利用できない人々は，情報やサービスへのアクセス機会を失う可能性がある。

③偽造や複製による権利侵害

　デジタル技術の進化により，画像・映像・音声などの偽造や複製が容易になった。これにより，人格権の侵害や詐欺行為，著作権侵害行為が増加している。こうし

た違法行為に至らないまでも，SNS などでは信頼性のない情報やコンテンツが拡散され，混乱や誤解を招くことが多い。

④デジタル中毒と精神的健康への影響

ソーシャルメディアやオンライン・エンターテインメントへの依存（デジタル中毒）が問題となっている。これにより，バーチャルとリアルのバランスが崩れ，精神的健康に悪影響を及ぼす可能性がある。

これらの問題点はデジタル文化が抱える脆弱性の一部である。これらの課題に対処するためには，適切なセキュリティ対策やデジタルリテラシーの向上，情報の信頼性を高める取り組みなどが求められる。

確認問題

1. ①〜⑩は語句の意味を日本語で書き，⑪〜⑳は和訳と対応する英語の語句を，頭文字を参考にして書き，空欄を完成させよう。（各1点×20）

/40点

① device 名 _____

② literature 名 _____

③ barely 副 _____

④ clue 名 _____

⑤ material 名 _____

⑥ cite 動 _____

⑦ rule 動 _____

⑧ dominate 動 _____

⑨ ensure 動 _____

⑩ preserve 動 _____

⑪ e_____ 形 外部の

⑫ w_____ o_____ 熟 全滅［壊滅］させる，根絶する

⑬ g_____ b_____ 熟 倒産する

⑭ i_____ 名 洞察，見識

⑮ a_____ 名 人類学者

⑯ c_____ 名 粘土

⑰ c_____ 形 共同社会の

⑱ h_____ 名 人類

⑲ a_____ 名 考古学

⑳ g_____ 名 統治

2. 次の［ ］の語句を並べ替えて，意味の通る英文を完成させよう。（各5点×2）

① Studying humanity's past [today / and / for / helps / the / navigate / us / future / seek].

人類の過去を研究することは，私たちが今日を生き抜き，未来を探求する上で役立つ。

② So the question then becomes, how do we [are / our / as / as / ensure / desiderata / preserved / that / possible / lives / and / digital / much]?

したがって，問題はどのようにすれば私たちのデジタルな生活と願望ができるだけ保護されるか，ということになる。

3. 次の英文を和訳してみよう。(10点)

This is because it is the small bits and pieces of a culture that we barely think about that often deliver the greatest clues and insights to archeologists and anthropologists studying past cultures.

ディクテーションしてみよう！

今回学習した英文に出てきた語句を，音声を聞いて＿＿＿＿＿に書き取ろう。

09　As we ❶＿＿＿＿＿＿＿＿＿＿＿＿＿＿＿ into the Cloud and on storage devices like external drives, tablets, and smartphones, we place bits and pieces of our culture there as well: music, art, literature, maps, videos, and photos.　These are all artifacts of our culture.　The problem with this data storage is that it is changing all the time and with every significant change ❷＿＿＿＿＿＿＿＿＿＿＿＿＿＿＿＿＿＿＿＿.　And if you think that keeping it all in the Cloud is the answer, it isn't.　Take a solar flare as an example.　If a major solar flare wipes out Amazon, Apple, Facebook, and other data centers, all will be lost.　❸＿＿＿＿＿＿＿＿＿＿＿＿＿＿＿＿ ＿＿＿＿＿＿, it is possible that the data it hosts will be lost.　The point is that there are many ways that we could lose our digital culture.

確認問題の答　1.　①装置，器具　　②文学　　③ほとんど〜ない　　④手がかり，ヒント
　　　⑤材料　　⑥挙げる，引用する　　⑦支配する，統治する　　⑧支配する，優位に立つ　　⑨確実にする
　　　⑩保存する，保護する　　⑪ external　　⑫ wipe out　　⑬ go bankrupt　　⑭ insight
　　　⑮ anthropologist　　⑯ clay　　⑰ communal　　⑱ humanity　　⑲ archaeology　　⑳ governance
　　2.　① helps us navigate today and seek for the future　（第2段落　第5文）
　　　② ensure that our digital lives and desiderata are preserved as much as possible　（第3段落　第5文）
　　3.　これは，私たちがほとんど考えない文化の小さな断片こそが，過去の文化を研究している考古学者や人類学者にこの上なく重要な手がかりや見識をもたらすからだ。　（第2段落　第2文）

ディクテーションしてみよう！の答　❶ put ever more of our lives
　❷ there is always the possibility of losing data　　❸ Or if one of these companies goes bankrupt

解答

問1	（ア）④	（イ）⑤	（ウ）②	（エ）①	（オ）⑧

問2	海の中で音は深さにより異なる速度で伝わり，海底で最も速いということ。

問3	（音を伝える）媒体の密度が高ければ高いほど，音波がそれを通過する際に分子がそれだけ速く振動する。

問4	クジラは絶えず，歌を少しずつ変化させていくが，鳥は時がたっても歌を変化させないということ。

問5	④

問6	⑤

解説

問1

（ア） in *one's* entirety「全体として，完全な状態で」。この in は【状態・形状】を表す。

（イ） 直後の the Cold War とセットで副詞句になっているので，前置詞を入れる。【特定の期間】を表す during を入れて，**During the Cold War**「冷戦中に」とすれば第1段落第3～5文（4～8行目）の内容に合う。

（ウ） 直後の listening につながる形を考える。「**時・条件・譲歩の副詞節中の〈S＋be動詞〉は省略可**」というルールがあるので，【時】を表す接続詞 **while** を入れ，While they（＝the scientists）were listening to the ocean, の they were が省略されたと考える。

（エ） **前置詞 across は「～を横切って，～を越えて」**の意味なので，travelled across hundreds, even thousands of miles で「数百マイル，場合によっては数千マイルの距離を伝わった」を意味することになる。

（オ） **under には【受動】の意味がある**（例 under control「支配されて」; under pressure「圧力を受けて」; under construction「建設中で」）。こ

こでは，**under threat** で「**脅かされて，脅威にさらされて**」の意味。

問2

this は原則として直前の文に指示内容がある。ここでは，**直前の文の後半の that 節を指す**と考える。なぜなら，前半は They knew that ... とあるので，「もともと知っていたこと」，後半は they also found that ... とあるので，「新たにわかったこと」である。そして，This may seem surprising, とあるので，「驚くべきこと」はどちらであるかを考えれば，当然，後半のみである。

問3

The denser the medium, the faster the molecules shake as the sound wave goes through it.

以下のポイントをおさえよう！

☑ 〈**The 比較級 ～，the 比較級 ...**〉は「**～すればするほど…**」の意味。「～」と「…」にはそれぞれ〈S + V〉が入るが，be 動詞はよく省略される。ここでは，the medium の後に is を補って考える。

☑ **as は接続詞**で，ここでは【**時**】を表すと考える。「**～が…する際に[ときに]**」の意味。

問4

「クジラと鳥が異なる」との記述は，第3段落第10文(34行目)に ... whales are very different from birds, ... とあるので，この前後の第8～11文(30～40行目)をまとめる。

クジラについては，underwent slow but continuous evolution(31行目)，subtle changes in the songs each year(32～33行目)などの記述から，「**歌が絶えず少しずつ変化する**」ことがわかる。

他方，**鳥**については，whose songs remain stable over time(35～36行目)という記述から，「**時を経ても歌が変化しない**」ことがわかる。

問5

下線部直後に so to speak「いわば」とあるので，became big が物理的に大きくなることを意味していないのは明らかである。よって②は不正解。では，どういう意味で「大きくなる」のかといえば，同段落の第2文の had great emotional power（44行目）から，人の心の中で大きな存在になるのだと理解できる。各選択肢の意味は，①「クジラが成熟した」，②「クジラが大きくなった」，③「クジラの数が増加した」，④「**クジラが大いに注目を引いた**」，⑤「クジラが長生きするようになった」。

問6

① 「海底の研究のために録音技術が十分に発達する以前から，研究者は長い間，クジラが互いにコミュニケーションをすると考えてきた」

▶ 研究者がクジラのコミュニケーションを取る声であるとわかった，との記述は第2段落（14～19行目）にあるが，「長い間そのように考えていた」との記述はない。なお，録音技術発達については第1段落第2文（2行目）に記述があり，それによってクジラの歌の全容がわかるという内容。研究者の考え方との関係は書かれていない。

② 「クジラの歌を何年間も徹底的に研究した結果，それが求愛の儀式と関係があることが明らかになった」

▶ このような記述はない。なお，第3段落第7文（28～30行目）により，クジラの歌はオスがメスを求めるような意図のものではないことがわかる。

③ 「メスのクジラはオスのクジラと全く異なる歌い方をする」

▶ そのような記述はない。また，第3段落第2文（22行目）によれば，少なくとも人間にわかっているクジラの歌は，オスしか歌わないことになる。

④ 「何人かの音楽家は水中で音楽を演奏することによりクジラに嫌がらせをすることを意図した」

▶ 第4段落最終文（46～49行目）と不一致。音楽家たちはクジラに敬意を表したかったのであり，嫌がらせをしたかったわけではない。また，水中で演奏したとは書かれていない。

⑤ 「**音楽はクジラの邪魔をすると考えられているため，もうクジラに向かって音楽を演奏することは許されていない**」

▶ 第4段落最終文（46～49行目）と一致するのでこれが正解。

第1段落

¹Sailors have long known that whales make strange musical noises. ²Yet it wasn't until recording techniques were developed that anyone could listen to whale songs in their entirety. ³It was, in fact, military science that first collected the evidence. ⁴During the Cold War, the US government conducted secret research into how sound travels underwater. ⁵The Americans were looking for ways to locate enemy submarines, and to hide their own. ⁶They knew that sound travels five times faster underwater than it does through the air, but they also found that it travels at different speeds in different layers of the ocean, fastest of all at the bottom. ⁷This may seem surprising, but as David Rothenberg explains: "The denser the medium, the faster the molecules shake as the sound wave goes through it."

→ p.39 文構造Check!

> 訳 ¹船乗りは，クジラが奇妙な音楽的な音声を発することを昔から知っていた。²しかし，録音技術が発達してからやっと，だれもがクジラの歌の全体像を聴くことができるようになった。³実は，最初に証拠を集めたのは軍事科学であった。⁴冷戦中，アメリカ政府は水中での音の伝わり方を密かに調査していた。⁵アメリカ政府は敵の潜水艦を見つけ，自らの潜水艦は隠しておく方法を探し求めていた。⁶彼らは，空気中と比べ，水中では音が5倍の速さで伝わることは知っていたが，海中の異なる深度において異なる速度で伝わり，海底で最も速いということも発見した。⁷これは意外に思われるかもしれないが，デービッド・ローゼンバーグの説明のとおり，「（音を伝える）媒体の密度が高ければ高いほど，音波がそれを通過する際に分子がそれだけ速く振動する」のである。

語句

sailor	名	船乗り，水夫
whale	名	クジラ
musical	形	音楽的な
yet	接	けれども，だが
recording	名	録音

technique	名	技術，技法
entirety	名	全体，全部，完全
▶ in *one*'s entirety		全体として，完全な状態で
military	形	軍隊の，軍事の
evidence	名	証拠

the Cold War	名	(米ソ間の)冷戦	submarine	名 潜水艦

the Cold War 名 (米ソ間の)冷戦
government 名 政府
conduct 動 (調査，実験などを)行う
research 名 研究，調査
travel 動 (光や音などが)伝わる[進む]
underwater 副 水中で／形 水中の
locate 動 探す，見つける
enemy 形 敵の

submarine 名 潜水艦
hide 動 隠す
layer 名 層
bottom 名 水底，海底
dense 形 濃い，高密度の
medium 名 媒体，媒介，媒質
molecule 名 分子
sound wave 名 音波

文構造Check!

Yet it wasn't (until recording techniques were developed)
　　　　　　　従接　　　　　S　　　　　　　　V

that anyone could listen to whale songs (in their entirety).
　　　S　　　　V　　　　　　O

▶ It is not until ～ that ... 「～してはじめて…」

It was, (in fact), military science that first collected the evidence.
　　　　　　　　　　S　　　　　　　V　　　O

▶ It was ～ that ... は強調構文。～(＝強調される部分)に移動している
military science が S，collected が V，the evidence が O。

　　　　　　　　　is 省略
　　　　　　　　　V
(The denser the medium), the faster the molecules shake
　　　C　　　　S　　　　　　　　　　　　S　　　　V

(as the sound wave goes (through it)).
　従接　　　S　　　　V

第2段落

¹While listening to the ocean, the scientists heard low moaning and rumbling noises that they gradually learned to identify (and dismiss) as the sound of living creatures. ²**These turned out to be**
→ p.40　文構造Check!

great whales communicating with one another in the deep sound channels, where their utterances travelled across hundreds, even thousands of miles.

語句

gradually	副	徐々に，だんだんに
identify	動	確認する
▶ **identify _A_ as _B_**		A が B だと確認する［わかる］
dismiss	動	退ける
▶ **dismiss _A_ as _B_**		A を B として退ける，問題にしない

creature	名	生物，動物
▶ **living creature**		生き物
turn out to be 〜	熟	結局〜だとわかる
deep	形	(声・音が)低い
channel	名	周波数帯
utterance	名	発声

文構造Check!

These turned out to be
S　　V

〈 great whales communicating (with one another) (in the deep sound channels)〉,
C　　S'　　　　V'

where their utterances travelled (across hundreds, even thousands of miles).
関副　　S　　　　V

▶ この文だけを見れば，communicating は現在分詞で whales を修飾しているとも考えられるが，These が直前の文の low moaning and rumbling noises を指すので，この解釈は無理がある。そこで，communicating を動名詞，great whales を動名詞の意味上の主語と考える。where は関係副詞で非制限用法。

第3段落

¹By listening to humpback whale songs through underwater microphones, scientists discovered that whales do not cry and moan randomly. ²The songs — always sung by males — had long-range structures, sometimes lasting for hours. ³They were shaped like any good musical composition, with themes, phrases, climaxes, resolution, and dying away. ⁴Moreover, the songs were repeated after a pause. ⁵They seemed to be transmitted to other whales living in the same area who sang them too. ⁶Different groups in other oceans had their own distinctive songs. ⁷The songs were too long and formal merely to be passing on simple information about females, food or the ocean floor. ⁸Strangest of all, they underwent slow but continuous evolution. **⁹Researchers who came back summer after summer noticed subtle changes in the songs each year, all the whales in the area picking up the changes.**
→ p.42　文構造Check!
¹⁰This means that whales are very different from birds, those other well-known singers of the natural world, whose songs remain stable over time. ¹¹Whereas today's nightingales may sound very similar to the ones that Shakespeare heard, a whale researcher will complain that the great whale singers of the 1970s have gone now, and that the music favored by today's youngsters is entirely different.

訳 ¹ザトウクジラの歌を水中マイクを通じて聴くことにより，科学者たちはクジラが無作為に叫んだりうめき声を出したりしているのではないということを発見した。²その歌は，常にオスが歌うのだが，時には数時間続くという遠大な構成になっていた。³それらの歌は優れた音楽の作曲と同様の形式になっており，テーマ，楽句，クライマックス，（不協和音の）解決，フェードアウトが含まれていた。⁴その上，その歌は中断した後に反復されていたのだ。⁵その歌はまた同じ海域に住み，同じ歌を歌うほかのクジラに伝えられているようであった。⁶ほかの海域にいる別のグループには彼ら特有の歌があった。⁷その歌は，メスやエサや海底についての単純な情報を単に伝えているにしては，長すぎるし，形式が整いすぎていた。⁸最も奇妙なことに，それらの歌はゆっくりだが絶え間ない発達を遂げていたのである。⁹夏ごとに戻ってくる研究者たちは，毎年クジラの歌に微妙な変化があり，その海域に住むすべてのクジラがその変化を身につけていることに気づいた。¹⁰このことは，

クジラが，自然界でもう１つの有名な歌い手である鳥とは非常に異なっていることを意味する。なぜなら，鳥の歌は時を経ても変化しないからである。[11]今日のナイチンゲールはシェークスピアが聞いていたナイチンゲールととても似た鳴き声をしている可能性があるのに対し，クジラの研究者は，1970年代の偉大なクジラの歌手は今では姿を消し，今日の若者クジラに好まれる音楽はまるで違っているのだ，と不平を言うことになる。

語句

microphone	名	マイク	
randomly	副	無作為に，でたらめに	
long-range	形	長期間にわたる	
structure	名	構造，構成	
last	動	続く，継続する	
shape	動	形作る，作る	
composition	名	作曲，曲	
die away	熟	(音が)次第に弱まり消えていく	
pause	名	中断，途切れ	
transmit	動	伝える	
distinctive	形	独特の，特有の	
formal	形	整然とした，規則的な	
merely	副	単に	
pass on ~	熟	～を伝える	

ocean floor	名	海底，海洋底	
undergo	動	経る，受ける	
＊活用：undergo-underwent-undergone			
continuous	形	絶え間ない	
evolution	名	進化，発達	
subtle	形	微妙な，わずかな	
pick up ~	熟	～を身につける	
well-known	形	有名な，よく知られた	
stable	形	不変の	
over time	熟	時がたつと，時とともに	
whereas	接	…する一方で，…であるのに	
nightingale	名	ナイチンゲール(ツグミ類の渡り鳥)	
favor	動	好む	
youngster	名	若者	
entirely	副	全く，すっかり	

文構造Check!

Researchers 〔 who came back (summer after summer)〕
S　　　　　関代　　　V

noticed subtle changes 〔 in the songs 〕(each year),
V　　　　O

(all the whales in the area picking up the changes).
　　　　S'　　　　　　　　　V'　　　　O'

▶ picking は現在分詞で，all ... changes は【付帯状況】を表す独立分詞構文になっている。all the whales in the area は picking up の意味上の主語として働く。

第4段落

¹Whales became big, so to speak, when endangered species caught our imagination in the 70s. ²The idea that the world's largest creatures were singing at the bottom of the ocean had great emotional power. ³Some musicians even went out in boats to play to them. ⁴Did the whales respond? ⁵The musicians thought so. ⁶It was all meant to be a homage, an inter-species get-together, but it had to stop when the Marine Mammal Protection Act forbade anyone from harassing the animals and classed music as a form of harassment.

訳 ¹70年代に絶滅危惧種が我々の想像力をとらえたとき、クジラはいわば大きな存在になった。²世界最大の生物が海底で歌を歌っているという考えは、感情に訴えかける大きな力を持っていた。³何人かの音楽家は、クジラに向かって演奏をするために、わざわざ船で海に出て行った。⁴クジラは反応したのであろうか。⁵その音楽家たちは、そのように思っていた。⁶それはもっぱら敬意を表し、異種間の親睦を図ることを意図したものであったが、海洋哺乳類保護法によりいかなる者も動物に嫌がらせをすることが禁じられ、音楽が嫌がらせの一形態であると分類されると、やめなくてはならなくなった。

語句

so to speak 熟 いわば
endangered 形 絶滅の危機にさらされた
imagination 名 想像（力）
emotional 形 感情的な，情緒的な
respond 動 反応する
homage 名 敬意，尊敬
inter-species 形 異種間の
　※ inter- ～「～の間の，～相互の」

get-together 名 親睦会，懇親会
forbid 動 禁じる
　＊活用：forbid-forbade-forbidden
harass 動 迷惑をかける，嫌がらせをする
class 動 分類する
　▶ class *A* as *B* A を B に分類する
form 名 形態，種類
harassment 名 迷惑行為，嫌がらせ

第5段落

[1]Some people warn that because of motorized shipping and seismic exploration of the ocean floor by oil companies, the seas are getting much noisier. [2]There is evidence that whales are trying to sing louder to make themselves heard; furthermore, recent sonar tests have been known to kill whales.

> **訳** [1]エンジンを搭載した船舶や，石油会社による海底の地震探査のせいで，海が以前よりずっと騒がしくなってきていると警告する人々もいる。[2]クジラが自分の声を届かせるために以前よりも大きな声で歌おうとしているという証拠もある。さらに，近年のソナーによるテストがクジラを殺してしまうこともわかってきた。

語句

warn	動	警告する
motorize	動	エンジンをつける
shipping	名	船舶
exploration	名	調査，探査
loud	副	大きな声で

make *one*self **heard**	熟	自分の声を聞いてもらう，声を届かせる
furthermore	副	さらに，その上
sonar	名	ソナー，水中音波探知機

第6段落

We know that whale songs are complex messages, but we still don't know what they mean or what we could learn from them, and now they may be under threat.

> **訳** クジラの歌が複雑なメッセージであることはわかっているが，その意味や，そこから何が学び取れるかは，いまだわかっていない。そして，その歌は今，脅威にさらされている。

語句

complex	形	複雑な

threat	名	脅威，脅かすもの
▶ **under threat**		脅威にさらされて，脅かされて

パラグラフ展開　英文全体の内容を把握しよう！

第1段落　主題の提示

クジラの歌

　船乗りは以前から知っていた

　　　→ 録音技術の発達により全容が明らかになる

　　　→ 冷戦中，軍事科学により証拠収集

第2段落

海から聞こえるうめき声のような音＝クジラのコミュニケーション

第3段落

クジラの歌に関する科学者による発見

　①でたらめに声を出しているのではない

　②音楽の作曲と同様の形式がある

　③中断を挟み反復される

　④同じ海域のほかのクジラに伝えられる

　⑤海域により独特の歌がある

　⑥歌は長く形式が整っている → 単純な情報の伝達ではない

　⑦ゆっくり絶え間なく変化 → 歌がずっと変化しない鳥とは違う

第4段落

クジラへの注目が高まる ← 絶滅危惧種への注目

音楽家はクジラに向けて音楽を演奏 → 法により禁じられる

第5段落

クジラを取り巻く環境

　①エンジン搭載の船舶

　②石油会社による地震探査

　③ソナー（水中音波探知機）によるテスト

第6段落

クジラの歌は脅威にさらされている

　クジラの歌(鳴き声)によるコミュニケーションを扱った英文。生物学系のテーマという点では、問題8の東北大学の英文と似ているが、本英文はそれほど理屈っぽくはなく、むしろ、たとえ話なども豊富で親しみやすい英文と言えるだろう。クジラのほか、類人猿や鳥、ミツバチなど、コミュニケーションを行うとみられる生物は多く、中には「言語」と呼ぶに値するものを持つ生物もいる。そうなると、ヒトとほかの動物とを分け隔てる点は何であるのか、究極的には、「人類とは?」という問いにもつながってくる。遺伝子工学が発達し、ヒトはチンパンジーとDNAの塩基配列では約99%同じであると判明してはいるが、一方でチンパンジーは赤ん坊と同じ言語環境に置かれても人間の言語を話すようにはならないとの報告もある。人間の種特異性とは何かという問いに対する関心は高まっており、入試問題にも多く取り上げられている。

確認問題

1. ①〜⑩は語句の意味を日本語で書き，⑪〜⑳は和訳と対応する英語の語句を，頭文字を参考にして書き，空欄を完成させよう。（各1点×20）

⏐ /40点

① submarine 名 [_____]

② layer 名 [_____]

③ creature 名 [_____]

④ transmit 動 [_____]

⑤ distinctive 形 [_____]

⑥ undergo 動 [_____]

⑦ evolution 名 [_____]

⑧ endangered 形 [_____]

⑨ harassment 名 [_____]

⑩ exploration 名 [_____]

⑪ [c_____] 動 （調査，実験などを）行う

⑫ [l_____] 動 探す，見つける

⑬ [i_____] A [a] B 熟 A が B だと確認する［わかる］

⑭ [s_____] 名 構造，構成

⑮ [l_____] 動 続く，継続する

⑯ [p_____] [o_____] ～ 熟 ～を伝える

⑰ [s_____] 形 微妙な，わずかな

⑱ [s_____] to [s_____] 熟 いわば

⑲ [i_____] 名 想像(力)

⑳ [w_____] 動 警告する

2. 次の[ ]の語句を並べ替えて，意味の通る英文を完成させよう。（各5点×2）

① The denser the medium, [as / the sound wave / the / faster / goes / shake / the molecules / through] it.

媒体の密度が高ければ高いほど，音波がそれを通過する際に分子がそれだけ速く振動する。

② There is evidence that whales [sing / themselves / louder / to / make / to / heard / are / trying].

クジラが自分の声を届かせるために，より大きな声で歌おうとしているという証拠もある。

3. 次の英文を和訳してみよう。(10点)

Yet it wasn't until recording techniques were developed that anyone could listen to whale songs in their entirety.

ディクテーションしてみよう！

今回学習した英文に出てきた語句を，音声を聞いて＿＿＿＿＿に書き取ろう。

16 Sailors have long known that whales make strange musical noises. Yet it wasn't until recording techniques were developed that anyone could listen to whale songs in their entirety. It was, in fact, military science ❶＿＿＿＿＿＿＿＿＿＿＿＿＿＿＿＿＿＿. During the Cold War, the US government conducted secret research into how sound travels underwater. The Americans were looking for ways to locate enemy submarines, and to hide their own. They knew that ❷＿＿＿＿＿＿＿＿＿＿＿＿＿＿＿＿ ＿＿＿＿＿＿ than it does through the air, but they also found that it travels at different speeds in different layers of the ocean, ❸＿＿＿＿＿＿＿＿＿ ＿＿＿. This may seem surprising, but as David Rothenberg explains: "The denser the medium, the faster the molecules shake as the sound wave goes through it."

17 While listening to the ocean, the scientists heard low moaning and rumbling noises that they gradually learned to identify (and dismiss) as the sound of living creatures. These turned out to be great whales ❹＿＿＿＿＿＿＿＿＿＿＿＿＿＿＿＿＿ in the deep sound channels, where their utterances travelled across hundreds, even thousands of miles.

確認問題の答

1. ①潜水艦　　②層　　③生物，動物　　④伝える　　⑤独特の，特有の
　　⑥経る，受ける　　⑦進化，発達　　⑧絶滅の危機にさらされた　　⑨迷惑行為，嫌がらせ
　　⑩調査，探査　　⑪conduct　　⑫locate　　⑬identify / as　　⑭structure　　⑮last　　⑯pass on
　　⑰subtle　　⑱so / speak　　⑲imagination　　⑳warn
2. ① the faster the molecules shake as the sound wave goes through　（第1段落　最終文）
　　② are trying to sing louder to make themselves heard　（第5段落　第2文）
3. しかし，録音技術が発達してからやっと，だれもがクジラの歌の全体像を聴くことができるようになった。
　　（第1段落　第2文）

ディクテーションしてみよう！の答

　　❶ that first collected the evidence
　　❷ sound travels five times faster underwater　　❸ fastest of all at the bottom
　　❹ communicating with one another

解答

問1 いくつかの科学的概念は我々の教育制度により大きく損なわれてきたので，皆が知っていると思っていて，実は知らない概念について説明する必要がある。

問2 学校教育により，実験とは退屈なもので，科学者が行うもので，日常生活とは無関係なものだと我々が学習してしまうこと。

(56字)

問3 しかし，自分の行動を実験とみなしておらず，データから慎重に推論する方法も知らない人は，それができる人と比べて，経験から学習することが下手なままであろう。

問4 薬の服用後に毎回注意深く結果を記録し，対照実験を行い，一度に1つの行動のみを変えることで複数の変数を混ぜないようにする。

(60字)

解説

問1

Some scientific concepts have been so ruined (by our education system)
　　　　　S　　　　　　　　　　V

(that it is necessary
　　仮S V　　C

⟨ to explain the ones
真S

〔that everyone thinks ⟨they know about and really don't⟩〕⟩).
　関代　　S　　　V　　O S　V②　　　　　　　　V②
　　　　　　　　　　　従接that省略　　know about省略
　　　　　　　　　　　　　　　　　　　等接

以下のポイントをおさえよう！

☑ **so ~ that ...**「とても～なので…」

☑ **ruin は動詞**で用いると「**破壊する，損なう，台なしにする**」の意味。

50

- ☑ that 以下は **it が仮主語**，**to explain 〜 が真主語**。
- ☑ the ones は the scientific concepts の代用。
- ☑ the ones の後の that は目的格の関係代名詞。この後の構造は，everyone thinks を挿入句的に考え，they know about の後に前置詞の目的語が欠け，さらに don't の後に know about の省略を補い，really don't（know about）の後にやはり前置詞の目的語が欠けている。thinks の O が欠けているわけではないので注意。

問2

　下線部(2)の this は，第2段落(4〜11行目)全体を指すものと考えられるが，60字以内では書き切れないので，第2段落で最も重要な部分に絞り込まなければならない。そこで，第2段落最終文(9行目)の文頭に **So があるのに注目し，これより前が「原因」，最終文が「結果」の関係**になっていると考える。もちろん，「原因」ではなく「結果」が problem「問題」であろうから，第2段落最終文をまとめることになる。ただ，これらは学校教育の問題点であるから，「学校(の授業)で」「学校教育により」などの言葉を補う。

問3

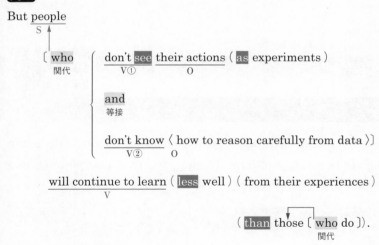

以下のポイントをおさえよう！
- ☑ **people が S，will continue to learn が V**。

☑ 関係代名詞 who の節は data まで。節の中では，don't see their actions as experiments と don't know how to reason carefully from data が and により並列されている。

☑ **see _A_ as _B_**「**A を B とみなす**」

☑ **reason は動詞**で用いると「**推論する，推理する**」の意味。

☑ **less ～ than ...** は「**…ほど～ない**」。**well** は「**うまく，よく**」の意味の副詞。そこで，「…ほど経験からうまく学習しない」が直訳。

☑ those who do は people who see their actions as experiments and know how to reason carefully from data の代用。

☑ **will continue to learn less well** の部分は，「うまく学習しないでいることを続ける」が直訳なので，「**うまく学習できないままである**」などとする。

問4

「処方薬」については第4段落。第4段落第2文後半(24行目)に【結果】を表す **so that** があり，この後に「副作用が出ても原因がわからない」とあるので，この文の前半に書かれている内容の逆のことをすれば原因がわかるはずである。

▼

それでは次に，段落ごとに詳しく見ていこう。

第1段落

Some scientific concepts have been so ruined by our education system that it is necessary to explain the ones that everyone thinks they know about and really don't.

訳 いくつかの科学的概念は我々の教育制度により大きく損なわれてきたので，皆が知っていると思っていて，実は知らない概念について説明する必要がある。

語句

scientific	形 科学的な	ruin	動 破壊する，損なう
concept	名 概念	education	名 教育

第2段落

¹We learn about experimentation in school.　²What we learn is that scientists conduct experiments, and in our high school labs if we copy exactly what they did, we will get the results they got.　³We learn about the experiments scientists do — usually about the physical and chemical properties of things — and we learn that they report their results in scientific journals.　⁴So, in effect, we learn that experimentation is boring, is something done by scientists, and has nothing to do with our daily lives.

訳　¹我々は実験の方法について学校で学ぶ。²我々が学ぶのは，科学者が実験を行い，彼らがやったことを高校の実験室で正確に模倣すれば，彼らと同じ結果が我々にも得られるということである。³我々は科学者が行う実験——通常は，物の物理的・化学的特性に関する実験——について学び，彼らがその結果を科学誌において発表していることも学ぶ。⁴したがって，事実上，我々が学ぶのは，実験作業が退屈であること，科学者により行われるものであること，我々の日常生活には無関係であること，なのだ。

語句

experimentation	名 実験方法，実験作業	**physical**	形 物理的な，物質的な
scientist	名 科学者	**chemical**	形 化学的な
conduct	動 （調査，実験などを）行う	**property**	名 特性，属性
experiment	名 実験／動 実験する	**report**	動 報告する
lab	名 実験室	**journal**	名 専門誌，定期刊行物
	＊laboratory の略語	▶ **scientific journal**	科学誌
copy	動 まねる，模倣する	**in effect**	熟 実際には，事実上は
exactly	副 正確に	**boring**	形 退屈な，つまらない
result	名 結果	**have nothing to do with ~**	
			熟 ～と関係がない

第3段落

¹And this is a problem.　²Experimentation is something done by everyone all the time.　³Babies experiment with what might be good to put in their mouths.　⁴Toddlers experiment with various behaviors to see what they can get away with.　⁵Teenagers experiment with

sex, drugs, and rock and roll. ⁶But because people don't really see these things as experiments or as ways of collecting evidence in support or refutation of hypotheses, they don't learn to think about experimentation as something they do constantly and thus need to learn to do better.

訳 ¹そして，この点が問題なのである。²実験は常にあらゆる人が行っていることなのである。³赤ん坊は何を口に入れてよいのかを実験する。⁴歩き始めたばかりの幼児は何がしかられずに済むのかを確かめようと，さまざまな行動を実験する。⁵十代の若者たちはセックスやドラッグやロックンロールに関して実験する。⁶だが，実際には，人々は，これらの事柄を実験としては，あるいは仮説を裏付けたり反証したりする際の証拠収集の方法としては考えていないので，実験について，自分が絶えずやっているのだから，もっとうまくやるようになる必要があることなのだ，とは考えるようにはならない。

語句

all the time 熟 常に，いつでも
toddler 名 (歩き始めの)幼児
get away with ～ 熟 ～をしても許される，
　　　　　　　　　　　　～の罰を免れる
see A as B 熟 A を B とみなす
evidence 名 証拠

in support of ～ 熟 ～を支持して，～を裏付けて
refutation 名 論破，反証
　▶ in refutation of ～ ～を反証して
hypothesis 名 仮説
constantly 副 絶えず，絶え間なく

第4段落

¹Every time we take a prescription drug, we are conducting an experiment. ²**But we don't carefully record the results after** <small>→ p.55 文構造Check!</small> **each dose, and we don't run controlled experiments, and we mix up the variables by not changing only one behavior at a time, so that when we suffer from side effects we can't figure out what might have been their true cause.** ³We do the same with personal relationships: When they go wrong, we can't figure out why, because the conditions are different in each one.

訳 ¹我々は処方薬を飲むたびに，実験を行っている。²しかし我々は毎回薬を服用した後に注意深く結果を記録せず，対照実験も行わず，一度に１つの行動のみを変えるということをしないことにより，さまざまな変数を混ぜ合わせてしまう。その結果，副作用に苦しんだとき，真の原因となりそうなものが何であったのか，理解できないのだ。³私たちは人間関係においても同じことをやってしまう。人間関係がうまくいかないとき，その理由が理解できないのは，それぞれの人間関係ごとに条件が異なるからである。

語句

prescription	名	処方箋
▶ prescription drug		処方薬
dose	名	（薬の）１回の服用量，一服
run	動	（実験，検査などを）行う
controlled experiment	名	対照実験
mix up	熟	混同する，混ぜ合わせる
behavior	名	行動
suffer from ～	熟	～に苦しむ
side effect	名	副作用
figure out ～	熟	～を理解する
go wrong	熟	うまくいかない
condition	名	条件

文構造Check!

But we don't carefully record the results (after each dose),
等接　S　　　　　　V　　　　　O

and we don't run controlled experiments,
等接　S　　V　　　　　O

and we mix up the variables (by not changing only one behavior (at a time)),
等接　S　V　　O　　　　　　　　V′　　　　　O′

(so that (when we suffer (from side effects))
従接　　従接　S　V

　　we can't figure out ⟨ what might have been their true cause ⟩).
　　S　　V　　　O 疑　　　V　　　　　C

▶ so that は【結果】を表す用法。「その結果…，だから…」の意味。

第5段落

Now, while it is difficult if not impossible to conduct controlled experiments in most aspects of our lives, it is possible to come to understand that we are indeed conducting an experiment when we take a new job, or try a new tactic in a game, or pick a school to attend — or when we try and figure out how someone is feeling or wonder why we ourselves feel as we do.

> 訳 さて，私たちの生活のほとんどの局面において対照実験を行うことは，不可能ではないとしても困難であるが，新しい仕事に就くとき，ゲームで新しい戦術を試すとき，入る学校を選択するとき，あるいは，だれかがどのように思っているかを理解しようとしたり，自分自身がなぜこのような気持ちになっているのだろうかと考えたりするときに，実は実験を行っているのだとわかるようになることは可能である。

語句

if not ~ 熟 ~ではないとしても	**indeed** 副 本当に，実際に
aspect 名 面，局面	**tactic** 名 作戦，戦術
	pick 動 選ぶ，選択する

第6段落

[1]Every aspect of life is an experiment that can be better understood if it is perceived in that way. [2]But because we don't recognize this, we fail to understand that we need to reason logically from evidence we gather, carefully consider the conditions under which our experiment has been conducted, and decide when and how we might run the experiment again with better results. [3]The scientific activity that surrounds experimentation is about thinking clearly in the face of evidence obtained from the experiment. [4]But people who don't see their actions as experiments and don't know how to reason carefully from data will continue to learn less well from their experiences than those who do.

訳 ¹生活のあらゆる面が実験なのであり，そのように認識すれば，その実験をよりよく理解できるのである。²しかし我々はこれを認識していないため，収集した証拠から論理的に推論したり，実験が行われた際の条件を慎重に考慮したり，よりよい結果を得られる実験をいつどのように再度行えばよいのかを決定したりする必要があることを理解することができないのだ。³実験を取り巻く科学的活動は，実験から得られた証拠に直面して明瞭に思考することに関わるものである。⁴しかし，自分の行動を実験とみなしておらず，データから慎重に推論する方法も知らない人は，それができる人と比べて，経験から学習することが下手なままであろう。

語句

perceive	動 理解する，認識する	condition	名 条件，状況
recognize	動 認識する，認める	activity	名 活動
fail to *do*	熟 ～できない，～しない	surround	動 取り巻く，密接に関連する
reason	動 推論する	in the face of ～	熟 ～に直面して
logically	副 論理的に	obtain	動 得る
		action	名 行動

第7段落

¹Most of us, having learned the word "experiment" in the context of a boring ninth-grade science class, have long since learned to discount science and experimentation as irrelevant to our lives. ²**If schools taught basic cognitive concepts, such as**
→ p.58 文構造Check!
experimentation in the context of everyday experience, instead of concentrating on algebra as a way of teaching people how to reason, then people would be much more effective at thinking about politics, child raising, personal relationships, business, and every other aspect of their daily lives.

訳 ¹我々の大半は，「実験」という語を第9学年の退屈な理科の授業という状況で学んだために，それ以降ずっと長い間，科学と実験を自分たちの生活に無関係なものとして軽視するようになってきてしまった。²もし学校が，推論の仕方を人々に教える手段として代数に重点を置く代わりに，日々の経験という状況の中での実験といったような基本的な認知的概念を教えるなら，人々は，政治，育児，人間関係，仕事，その他日常生活のあらゆる局面についてずっと効果的に考えるようになるだろう。

context	名	背景，状況
discount	動	軽視する
irrelevant	形	無関係な
instead of ～	熟	～の代わりに，～ではなくて

concentrate on ～	熟	～に集中する，～に専念する
effective	形	効果的な
politics	名	政治
child raising	名	子育て，育児

文構造Check!

(If schools taught basic cognitive concepts,
従接　S　　V　　　　　O

〔 such as experimentation 〔 in the context of everyday experience 〕〕,

(instead of concentrating on algebra (as a way of teaching people
V′　　　O′

how to reason))),
O′

then people would be much more effective
　　　S　　　V　　　　　C

(at thinking about

① politics,

② child raising,

③ personal relationships,

④ business,

and
等接

⑤ every other aspect of their daily lives).

▶ If 節中で過去形 taught，主節で would be が使われているので，【仮定法過去】（現在の事実に反する仮定）のパターン。then は If 節の内容を受けて主節が始まることを示す働き。

パラグラフ展開　英文全体の内容を把握しよう！

第1段落 導入

教育制度によって破壊された科学的概念

第2段落 主題の提示

「実験」→ 科学者が行うもの，日常生活と無関係，と思われている

第3段落 筆者の主張

「実験」→ だれもが常に行うもの

例 ①赤ん坊　　②歩き始めの幼児　　③十代の若者

第4段落 具体例

④処方薬　　⑤人間関係

第5段落 具体例

⑥新しい仕事　　⑦ゲームの戦略　　⑧学校選択

第6段落 筆者の主張

生活のあらゆる面が実験

⟷ 人々はそれがわかっていないから学習が不十分

第7段落

実験を日常生活と無関係だと思わせている学校教育への批判

テーマ解説

　英文の書き出しから，科学における実験がテーマだと思うかもしれないが，実際には「実験的手法」を日常生活に活用すべきであるとする内容で，科学的なテーマを扱ったものではない。とはいえ，control(led) experiment「対照実験（＝ある条件の効果を調べるために，その条件以外のほかの条件をすべて同じにして行う実験）」という概念を知っていると，理解しやすい内容である。

確認問題

1. ①〜⑩は語句の意味を日本語で書き，⑪〜⑳は和訳と対応する英語の語句を，頭文字を参考にして書き，空欄を完成させよう。（各1点×20）

① physical	形	
② chemical	形	
③ property	名	
④ evidence	名	
⑤ prescription	名	
⑥ tactic	名	
⑦ perceive	動	
⑧ recognize	動	
⑨ logically	副	
⑩ irrelevant	形	

⑪ i ___ e ___ 　熟　実際には，事実上は

⑫ h ___ n ___ to d ___ w ___ 〜　熟　〜と関係がない

⑬ s ___ *A* a ___ *B*　熟　AをBとみなす

⑭ in s ___ o ___ 〜　熟　〜を支持して，〜を裏付けて

⑮ s ___ f ___ 〜　熟　〜に苦しむ

⑯ f ___ o ___ 〜　熟　〜を理解する

⑰ f ___ t ___ *do*　熟　〜できない，〜しない

⑱ o ___ 　動　得る

⑲ e ___ 　形　効果的な

⑳ p ___ 　名　政治

2. 次の［　］の語句を並べ替えて，意味の通る英文を完成させよう。（各5点×2）

① [what / is / conduct / scientists / learn / that / we / experiments], and in our high school labs if we copy exactly what they did, we will get the results they got.

我々が学ぶのは，科学者が実験を行い，彼らがやったことを高校の実験室で正確に模倣すれば，彼らと同じ結果が我々にも得られるということである。

② Now, [while / conduct / to / is / it / impossible / not / if / difficult / experiments / controlled] in most aspects of our lives, it is possible to come to understand that we are indeed conducting an experiment when we take a new job.

さて，私たちの生活のほとんどの局面において対照実験を行うことは，不可能ではないとしても困難であるが，新しい仕事に就くときに，実は実験を行っているのだとわかるようになることは可能である。

3. 次の英文を和訳してみよう。（10 点）

Some scientific concepts have been so ruined by our education system that it is necessary to explain the ones that everyone thinks they know about and really don't.

ディクテーションしてみよう！

今回学習した英文に出てきた語句を，音声を聞いて＿＿＿＿に書き取ろう。

25　Some scientific concepts have been ❶＿＿＿＿＿＿＿＿＿＿＿＿＿＿＿ ＿＿＿＿＿ that it is necessary to explain the ones that everyone thinks they know about and really don't.

26　We learn about experimentation in school. What we learn is that scientists conduct experiments, and in our high school labs if we copy exactly what they did, we will get the results they got. We learn about the experiments scientists do — usually about ❷＿＿＿＿＿＿＿＿＿＿＿＿＿ ＿＿＿＿＿＿＿＿＿＿ — and we learn that they report their results in scientific journals. So, in effect, we learn that experimentation is boring, is something done by scientists, and ❸＿＿＿＿＿＿＿＿＿＿＿＿＿＿＿＿＿.

27   And this is a problem.   Experimentation is something done by everyone all the time. Babies experiment with ❹ _____ _____. Toddlers experiment with various behaviors to see what they can get away with. Teenagers experiment with sex, drugs, and rock and roll. But because people don't really see these things as experiments or as ways of collecting evidence in support or refutation of hypotheses, they don't learn to think about experimentation as something they do constantly and ❺ _____.

解 答

問1	人間は一般に認識されているよりもはるかに不合理な行動をしがちであるということ。
問2	②
問3	④
問4	人間はプライミング効果により自分の動作に無意識で影響されるが，実験で学生は賛成を意味する首を縦に振る動作をしたから。 （58字）
問5	「衝動買い」として知られているような行為を促進するという目的。
問6	①
問7	①，②

解 説

問1

　代名詞 this は原則として直前の文の一部または全部を指す。第2段落第1文(14行目)の this は，直前の段落の一部または全部を指すこともある。ここでは，the influence of words がその一例となるように考える。また，第1段落最終文(11〜12行目)に psychologists have shown in experimental studies that …「心理学者が実験に基づく研究で…ことを示してきた」とあり，第2段落では，そのことを立証するための，学生を使った実験(20〜33行目)について述べられているので，12行目の that 以下の内容が this の指示内容と考えられる。

問2

　下線部(2)直後に suggested by the words「それらの単語によって示唆されていた」とあり，この the words は第2段落第7文の 'retirement', 'wrinkle', 'grey', 'slow' and 'pension'(25行目)を指すと考えられる。そして，第2段落第7文で，これらの語は②the elderly を連想させる(which are normally

63

associated with the elderly)（24 行目）とある。

空欄**(3)**を含む英文の前半で，「学生たちの半分は…(Half of the students …)」とあるので，**「もう片方の半分」の意味にする**。「もう１つの～」は，全体が２者の場合は the other，３者以上の場合は another となる。ここでは**④ the other** が正解。

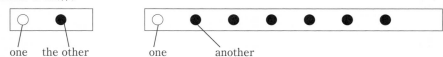

問4

下線部の意味は「首を上下させた学生たちのほうが，ヘッドフォンで聞いた意見に賛成する可能性が高かった」である。その理由としては，以下のように整理できる。

(1) 前提：プライミング効果(先行する刺激により，無意識であとの言動が影響を受ける効果)は自らのジェスチャーによっても生じる。＊第３段落第１，２文(34 ～ 35 行目)参照。

(2) この実験に当てはめると…

うなずくこと(首を縦に振ること)は「イエス(賛成)」を意味する。＊第３段落第４文(36 ～ 37 行目)参照。

⇒被験者の学生はある意見を聞きながら首を縦に振るよう求められた。＊同段落第７文(43 行目)参照。

⇒プライミング効果により，その意見に賛成するよう影響された。＊同段落第８文(45 ～ 47 行目)参照。

問5

this は原則として直前の文に指示内容がある。aim は「目的，目標」の意味。直前の文に**【目的】を表す副詞用法の不定詞**(to encourage what is known as 'impulse buying')があるので，この部分を書けばよい。

問6

go a long way は「とても役立つ，大いに効果がある」の意味。この語句を知らなくても，文脈から推測可能。人間は暗示による影響を免れないとしても，

行動を起こす前の self-reflection「自らを省みること」はどのような意味を持つのか，と考える。よって，① **be helpful**「役に立つ」が正解である。

問7

① 「人間の行動のほとんどすべての側面が本能的衝動により実際に支配されている」

▶ 第1段落第2文後半(4行目)と不一致。人間は，本能に従う動物と対比されており，「衝動を抑制する能力を持つ」とある。

② 「現代人は，自分が18世紀の人々よりもはるかに理性的だと思っている」

▶ このような記述はない。「18世紀」については，第1段落第3文(6行目)に啓蒙主義運動における理性の重要性についての言及があるが，この選択肢のような比較はなされていない。

③ 「人々はあまり明示的でない微妙な信号に容易に影響される」

▶ 第4段落第1文後半(51〜52行目)と一致。また，第2，3段落(14〜49行目)の実験結果もこの選択肢の内容に一致する。

④ 「前もって関連する語を示されると，より容易にそれらの語を認識できる」

▶ 第2段落第2，3文(14〜19行目)の例がこの選択肢の内容に一致する。

⑤ 「身体的行動は，自分が耳にした意見に対する態度に影響するかもしれない」

▶ 第3段落第5文以降(38〜49行目)で紹介されている実験とその結果がこの選択肢の内容に一致する。

⑥ 「18世紀の西欧の人々は人間の持つ理性の力の価値を強く信じていた」

▶ 第1段落第3文(6〜7行目)には，理性が当時のヨーロッパの啓蒙主義運動にとって重要であったとの記述がある。believe in 〜 は「〜の価値を信じる」の意味であり，理性の価値を信じることと，理性が重要な意味を持っていたことは，おおむね一致していると言える。

第1段落

[1]It has long been thought that one of the characteristics which separate humans from other animals is the ability to reason. [2]Whereas animals are slaves to their instincts, such as hunger, thirst, fear and the need to reproduce, humans have the capacity to control their urges and reflect upon their feelings. [3]Promotion of the use of reason was central to the Enlightenment movement in 18th century Europe. **[4]The ability to think problems through logically is something on which Western civilizations have prided themselves.** → p.67 文構造Check! [5]However, while it is certainly true that humans possess the capacity to employ logic in problem solving and in making good decisions, psychologists have shown in experimental studies that humans are likely to act irrationally far more often than is commonly perceived.

訳 [1]人間を動物と分け隔てている特徴の1つは，論理的に思考する能力である，と長らく考えられてきた。[2]動物は飢えやのどの渇き，恐怖や繁殖の必要といった本能に盲目的に従うのに対し，人間は欲望を抑制し，自分の感情をじっくり考える能力を持っている。[3]理性を働かせることを奨励するのが18世紀ヨーロッパの啓蒙主義運動において中心的であった。[4]さまざまな問題を論理的に考え抜くという能力は西洋文明が誇りを持ってきた事柄である。[5]しかし，確かに人間は，問題解決やよい決断を行う際に論理を用いる能力を有するのだが，心理学者たちは人間が一般に認識されているよりもはるかに不合理な行動をしがちであるということを，実験に基づく研究で示してきた。

語句

characteristic	名 特徴，特色	**reason**	動 論理的に考える，推論する／
separate	動 分け隔てる，区別する		名 理性，思考力
▶ **separate** *A* **from** *B*	A を B と区別する [分ける]	**whereas**	接 …だけれども，…の一方で
		slave	名 奴隷，盲目的に従う人
ability	名 能力	**instinct**	名 本能
		hunger	名 飢え，空腹

thirst	名 のどの渇き	**certainly**	副 確かに
reproduce	動 繁殖する	**possess**	動 所有する，持っている
capacity	名 能力	**employ**	動 使う，利用する
urge	名 衝動，欲望	**logic**	名 論理，推論
reflect upon[on] ~	熟 ~をよく考える，~を熟考する	**decision**	名 決定，決断
		▶ **make a decision** 決定する	
promotion	名 促進，奨励	**psychologist**	名 心理学者
central	形 中心的な，主要な	**experimental**	形 実験に基づく
enlightenment	名 啓発，教化	**be likely to** *do*	熟 ~する可能性が高い，~しそうだ
▶ **the Enlightenment** 啓蒙主義			
movement	名 運動，活動	**act**	動 振る舞う，行動する
think ~ **through**	熟 ~を考え抜く	**irrationally**	副 不合理に
logically	副 論理的に	**commonly**	副 一般的に，ふつうに
civilization	名 文明	**perceive**	動 認識する，理解する
pride *one*self on ~	熟 ~を誇りに思う		

文構造Check!

The ability〔 to think problems through logically 〕
S   ┗━━━ O′ ━━━V′━━━┛

is something
V C ↑

　　〔 on which Western civilizations have prided themselves 〕.
　　　関代　　　　S　　　　　　　V　　　　　O

....

▶ pride *one*self on ~ で「~に誇りを持つ」。ここでは，on ~ = on which で，この「前置詞＋関係代名詞」がセットで関係詞節の先頭に移動している点に注意。... something which Western civilizations have prided themselves on のように，関係詞のみを節の先頭に移動することも可。

第2段落

　　¹One example of this is the influence of words. ²If you have recently read or heard someone say the word 'eat', then you will be

more likely to use a 'u' rather than an 'a' to fill in the blank in the combination: 'so_p'. ³You will also be better able to recognize the word 'soup' when 'soup' is whispered to you than if you had not just been exposed to the idea of 'eating'. ⁴Words can also influence our physical actions. ⁵In a famous experiment, a group of American university students were told to make a sentence using a set of words presented to them. ⁶They were divided into two groups. ⁷One group was given a word list containing words which are normally associated with the elderly, such as 'retirement', 'wrinkle', 'grey', 'slow' and 'pension', while the list given to the other group contained no such words. ⁸When the students had finished their task, they were told to change rooms. ⁹The researchers found that the students who had been working with the set of words associated with old age walked more slowly than the other group. **¹⁰The word 'old' was not used, and all the students said in the interview after the experiment that they were unaware of the theme suggested by the words.** ¹¹Their behaviour had been influenced unconsciously.

→ p.69　文構造Check!

訳 ¹この１つの例は，言葉の影響である。²もし最近 'eat' という語を読んだり，だれかが言うのを聞いたりしていたら，'so_p' という連結の中の空欄を埋めるのに，'a' よりむしろ 'u' を使う可能性が高いであろう。³また，'eating'（食べる）という概念に触れ（させられ）たばかりでない場合と比べ，'soup' と小声で言われたときのほうが 'soup' という語を認識することがよりよくできるであろう。⁴言葉は私たちの身体的行動にも影響を及ぼし得る。⁵ある有名な実験で，アメリカの大学生のあるグループが，彼らに示された一連の言葉を用いて文を作るようにと言われた。⁶彼らは２つのグループに分けられた。⁷１つのグループは 'retirement'（退職），'wrinkle'（しわ），'grey'（白髪交じりの），'slow'（遅い），'pension'（年金）といった，通常は高齢者を連想させるような語を含む単語リストを与えられた。他方，もう１つのグループに与えられたリストにはそのような語が含まれていなかった。⁸学生たちは作業を終えたとき，部屋を変えるように言われた。⁹老齢を連想させる一連の語を用いて作業を行った学生たちが，他方のグループに比べてゆっくりと歩くことに研究者たちは気づいた。¹⁰'old' という語は使われなかったし，実験後のインタビューで学生たち全員が，それらの単語によって示唆されていたテーマに気づかなかったと言った。¹¹彼らの行動は無意識のうちに影響されていたのである。

語句

influence	名	影響／動 影響する
recently	副	最近
A* rather than *B	熟	B よりむしろ A
fill in ～	熟	～を埋める，～に書き入れる
blank	名	空欄
combination	名	連結，組み合わせ
recognize	動	認識する，判別する
whisper	動	ささやく，小声で言う
expose *A* to *B*	熟	A を B にさらす［触れさせる］
physical	形	身体的な，物理的な
action	名	行動，活動
experiment	名	実験
sentence	名	文
a set of ～	熟	一連の～，一群の～
present	動	提示する，示す
divide *A* into *B*	熟	A を B に分ける［分割する］
contain	動	含む
normally	副	通常は，ふつうは
associate *A* with *B*	熟	A を B と結びつけて考える，A から B を連想する
elderly	形	年配の，年老いた
retirement	名	退職，引退
wrinkle	名	(顔の)しわ
grey	形	白髪交じりの
pension	名	年金
task	名	作業，任務
researcher	名	研究者
be unaware of ～	熟	～に気づかない
theme	名	テーマ，主題
suggest	動	示唆する
behaviour	名	行動
unconsciously	副	無意識に

文構造Check!

The word 'old' was not used,
S　　　　　　V

and
等接

all the students said (in the interview 〔 after the experiment 〕)
S　　　　　　V

〈 that they were unaware (of the theme 〔 suggested by the words 〕)〉.
O従接　S　V　C

▶ and 以下の部分は all the students が S，said が V。この後に in the interview と after the experiment という 2 つの前置詞句が挟まって，that 節が O となる。このように V と O の間に修飾語句が挟まると構造が取りにくいので注意しよう。

¹The phenomenon described above is known in psychology as 'priming'. ²It can also be produced through your own gestures. ³This is because gestures are also a form of communication. ⁴For example, nodding means 'yes' and shaking the head means 'no'. ⁵To demonstrate how 'priming' may also apply to gestures, American university students in another experiment were given a set of headphones to wear. ⁶An opinion taken from a radio show was played through the headphones and the students were instructed to check for sound problems by moving their heads. ⁷Half of the students were asked to nod their heads up and down, while the other half were asked to shake their heads from side to side. ⁸The experimenters found that the students who nodded their heads up and down were more likely to agree with the opinion which they had heard through the headphones. **⁹This contrasted with the group that shook their heads, who were more likely to disagree.**

→ p.71 文構造Check!

訳 ¹上で述べた現象は，心理学においては「プライミング効果」として知られている。²それは，自らのジェスチャーによっても創り出すことが可能である。³これは，ジェスチャーもコミュニケーションの一形態だからである。⁴例えば，うなずくことは 'yes'（はい）を，首を横に振るのは 'no'（いいえ）を意味する。⁵「プライミング効果」がジェスチャーにも当てはまり得る様子を明らかにするために，別の実験において，アメリカの大学生たちがヘッドフォン一式を装着するようにと与えられた。⁶あるラジオ番組から取り出されたある意見が，ヘッドフォンを通じて再生され，学生たちは首を動かすことで音声の問題がないかどうかチェックするよう指示された。⁷学生の半数は首を上下させるよう求められ，他方，残りの半数は首を左右に振るように求められた。⁸実験者は，首を上下させた学生たちのほうが，ヘッドフォンで聞いた意見に賛成する可能性が高いということがわかった。⁹これは，首を横に振った学生たちのグループとは対照的であった。彼らは意見に反対する可能性がより高かったのだ。

語句

phenomenon	名 現象	**psychology**	名 心理学
describe	動 説明する，述べる	priming	名 プライミング（効果）
above	副 上で，前述の	**produce**	動 生み出す，もたらす
		form	名 形式，形態

nod	動 うなずく	**check for ~** 熟 ~がないかどうかを調べる
demonstrate	動 明らかに示す，証明する	**up and down** 熟 上下に
apply to ~	熟 ~に当てはまる	**side to side** 熟 左右に
headphone	名 ヘッドフォン	**contrast with ~** 熟 ~と対照的である
play	動 (音楽を)再生する[流す]	**disagree** 動 反対する
instruct	動 指示する	

文構造Check!

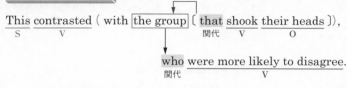

▶ who は the group を先行詞とする関係代名詞で，非制限用法。

第4段落

¹While no one would argue that humans are completely irrational, we are open to suggestion far more than we would like to believe. ²**We should therefore be aware of this when taking important decisions, especially if someone is actively trying to influence the outcome, such as in advertizing, or even when in supermarkets.** → p.73 文構造Check! ³For example, the interiors of these shops are often designed by psychologists to encourage what is known as 'impulse buying'. ⁴The use of lighting to display certain products and the physical placement of goods are designed with this aim in mind. ⁵It is no accident that comfort foods such as sweets and chocolates are frequently displayed at the checkout counter, where people have to wait in line. ⁶It may be impossible to make ourselves immune to all suggestion, but a little self-reflection before we act may go a long way.

¹人間が完全に不合理なものであると主張する人はいないであろうが，我々は自分が信じたく思うよりもはるかに暗示にかかりやすい。²したがって我々は重要な決断をするとき，特に，広告のように，あるいはまたスーパーマーケットにいるときのように，だれかが積極的に結果に影響を及ぼそうとしているような場合には，このことを意識しておくべきなのだ。³例えば，こういった店舗の内装は，「衝動買い」として知られているような行為を促進するために，心理学者によって設計されていることが多い。⁴一定の製品を展示するための照明の利用や，商品の物理的な配置は，このような目的を考えながら設計されている。⁵砂糖菓子やチョコレートのような口当たりのよい食品がレジの所に陳列されていることが多いのは偶然ではない。レジでは人々が一列に並んで待たなければならないからである。⁶あらゆる暗示に影響されないようにすることは不可能かもしれないが，行動する前にちょっとでも自己を省みると大いに役立つかもしれない。

語 句

argue	動	主張する
completely	副	完全に，全く
irrational	形	不合理な
be open to ～	熟	～を受けやすい
suggestion	名	示唆，暗示
therefore	副	それゆえに，したがって
be aware of ～	熟	～に気づいて，～を意識して
especially	副	特に，とりわけ
actively	副	積極的に
outcome	名	結果，結論，成果
advertizing	名	宣伝，広告
interior	名	内部，室内
design	動	設計する
encourage	動	促進する，助長する
impulse	名	衝動
▶ **impulse buying**		衝動買い
lighting	名	照明，採光
display	動	展示する，陳列する
certain	形	一定の，何らかの
product	名	製品
placement	名	配置
goods	名	商品，品物
with ～ in mind	熟	～を考慮に入れて，～を念頭に置いて
aim	名	目的
accident	名	偶然
comfort	名	安楽，安らぎ
sweet	名	甘い菓子，砂糖菓子
frequently	副	頻繁に
checkout counter	名	(店の)レジ
in line	熟	一列になって
immune	形	反応を示さない，影響を受けない
self-reflection	名	内省，自己を省みること
go a long way	熟	とても役立つ，大いに効果がある

文構造Check!

We should therefore be aware (of this)
S ～～～～～～～～～～～ V ～～～ C

(when [we are 省略] taking important decisions,
従接   S (V) V   O

　(especially if someone is actively trying to influence the outcome,
　①   従接 S   V   O

　　　　　　　　　　　　　　　　　　　　(such as in advertizing)),

　or
　等接

(even when [we are 省略] (in supermarkets))).
②   従接 S (V)

▶ when taking ... は when we are taking の we are が省略されていると
考える。時・条件・譲歩の副詞節中の〈S + be〉は省略できる場合がある。even
when ... の部分も同様。or が並列するのは，especially if ... in advertizing
と even when in supermarkets であり，such as in advertizing の部分は
if ... outcome の具体例を示している。

第1段落 導入

従来の考え方：人間と動物の違いは理性の有無。人間は理性的

↕

筆者の考え方：人間も理性的でない行動をとる

第2段落 具体例

人間は言葉による影響を受ける

①見たり聞いたりした語により，質問に対する答えが影響される（＝心理的な影響）

②老齢を連想させる言葉のリストを与えられたグループは無意識のうちに動きが緩慢になる（＝身体的な影響）

第3段落 具体例の説明

「プライミング効果」について

第2段落 のような影響を「プライミング効果」と呼ぶ

↓

ジェスチャーによっても「プライミング効果」は生じる

例 首を縦に振ったり横に振ったりするジェスチャーをしたところ，意見に対する賛否に影響が出た

第4段落 結論

人間は暗示にかかりやすい

↓

決断をするときには注意が必要

例 店の商品は衝動買いを助長するような配列になっている

テーマ解説

人間の心理に関する英文。プライミング効果（事前にある事柄を見聞きしたときに，あとの記憶や言動がそれに影響される現象）を，具体例を通じてわかりやすく解説している。プライミング効果は無意識的なものであるのが特徴。心理学的な現象について，実験を通じて検証するという内容の英文は，入試問題に多く見られる。

確認問題

1. ①〜⑩は語句の意味を日本語で書き，⑪〜⑳は和訳と対応する英語の語句を，頭文字を参考にして書き，空欄を完成させよう。（各1点×20）

/40点

① reproduce　動
② irrationally　副
③ expose A to B　熟
④ associate A with B　熟
⑤ pension　名
⑥ psychology　名
⑦ demonstrate　動
⑧ encourage　動
⑨ impulse　名
⑩ frequently　副
⑪ c_____　名　特徴，特色
⑫ i_____　名　本能
⑬ r_____ u_____ ～　熟　～をよく考える，～を熟考する
⑭ p_____　動　所有する，持っている
⑮ in_____　名　影響／動　影響する
⑯ d_____ A i_____ B　熟　AをBに分ける[分割する]
⑰ b_____　名　行動
⑱ n_____　動　うなずく
⑲ c_____ w_____ ～　熟　～と対照的である
⑳ o_____　名　結果，結論，成果

2. 次の[ ]の語句を並べ替えて，意味の通る英文を完成させよう。（各5点×2）

① The ability to think problems through logically is [Western / civilizations / on / something / have / which / prided] themselves.
さまざまな問題を論理的に考え抜くという能力は西洋文明が誇りを持ってきた事柄である。

75

② [to / make / it / impossible / may / to / be / ourselves / immune] all suggestion, but a little self-reflection before we act may go a long way.

あらゆる暗示に影響されないようにすることは不可能かもしれないが，行動する前にちょっとでも自己を省みると大いに役立つかもしれない。

3. 次の英文を和訳してみよう。（10点）

It has long been thought that one of the characteristics which separate humans from other animals is the ability to reason.

ディクテーションしてみよう！

今回学習した英文に出てきた語句を，音声を聞いて＿＿＿＿＿に書き取ろう。

32   It has long been thought that one of the characteristics which separate humans from other animals is ❶＿＿＿＿＿＿＿＿＿＿. Whereas animals are slaves to their instincts, such as hunger, thirst, fear and the need to reproduce, humans have the capacity to ❷＿＿＿＿＿＿＿＿＿＿
＿＿＿＿＿＿＿＿＿＿. Promotion of the use of reason was central to the Enlightenment movement in 18th century Europe. The ability to think problems through logically is something on which Western civilizations have prided themselves. However, while it is certainly true that humans possess the capacity to employ logic in problem solving and in making good decisions, ❸＿＿＿＿＿＿＿＿＿＿＿＿＿＿＿ that humans are likely to act irrationally far more often than is commonly perceived.

確認問題の答   **1.** ①繁殖する   ②不合理に   ③ A を B にさらす[触れさせる]
④ A を B と結びつけて考える，A から B を連想する   ⑤年金   ⑥心理学
⑦明らかに示す，証明する   ⑧促進する，助長する   ⑨衝動   ⑩頻繁に   ⑪ characteristic
⑫ instinct   ⑬ reflect upon   ⑭ possess   ⑮ influence   ⑯ divide / into
⑰ behavior [behaviour]   ⑱ nod   ⑲ contrast with   ⑳ outcome
2. ① something on which Western civilizations have prided （第 1 段落 第 4 文）
  ② It may be impossible to make ourselves immune to （第 4 段落 最終文）
3. 人間を動物と分け隔てている特徴の 1 つは，論理的に思考する能力である，と長らく考えられてきた。   （第
1 段落 第 1 文）

ディクテーションしてみよう！の答   ❶ the ability to reason
  ❷ control their urges and reflect upon their feelings
  ❸ psychologists have shown in experimental studies

解 答

問1 水中の塩分濃度に対する耐性

問2 海からの絶え間ない水分の蒸発こそが，その後凝縮して陸に降雨をもたらし，今度はその降雨が原因で，海は何十億年にわたって塩分を多く含むようになった。

問3 広範囲の塩分濃度への耐性を持つ魚が，淡水と海水を行き来することで外部の寄生虫を排除することができること。

塩分濃度が広範囲にわたる生息場所は，新しいえさや豊富なえさ，捕食者からの逃避手段，さらには安定した水温を提供してくれること。

問4 Vertebrate animals first evolved when the ocean was approximately one quarter as salty as it is today. As the ocean became saltier due to evaporation and rainfall on the land, several groups of vertebrates such as birds, mammals, reptiles and amphibians left the ocean to inhabit the land, while fish remained in the ocean. Vertebrates which chose to live on the land drank freshwater and took in salts from food to maintain their blood salt concentrations. On the other hand, fish evolved mechanisms to adapt to their different habitats (marine, fresh, and brackish water). For example, they developed the gills or altered kidney function.

（脊椎動物は最初，海が今日の約4分の1の塩分濃度であったころに進化した。海の塩分濃度が蒸発や降雨のせいで上昇するにつれて，鳥類・ほ乳類・は虫類・両生類といった，いくつかの脊椎動物のグループが，陸に住むために海を去り，他方，魚類は海に残った。陸に住むことを選んだ脊椎動物は，血中塩分濃度を維持するために，真水を飲み，食べ物から塩分を摂取した。他方，魚類は異なる生息場所（海水，淡水，汽水）に適応するための仕組みを発達させた。例えば，えらを発達させたり腎臓の機能を変えたりした。）

問1

　魚は salinity tolerance に従って分類される，という**(1)**を含む記述の後にその内容が具体化されている。第1段落第3文(4〜7行目)で狭い範囲の salinity にしか耐えられない魚，第2段落第1文(9〜10行目)で広い範囲の salinity に耐えられる魚について，具体例も挙げて説明されている。なお，salinity は salt の，tolerance は tolerate の派生語であることをスペルから見抜きたい。

問2

It was the constant evaporation of water〔from the ocean〕
　　　　　　　　　　　　　S

that then condensed (to cause rainfall〔on the land〕),
　　　　　V　　　　　　　 V′　　 O′

which (in turn), caused the ocean to become salty (over several billion years).
関代　　　　　　　　　V　　　 O　　 to become salty

以下のポイントをおさえよう！

☑ **It was 〜 that ... は強調構文**。「…するのは〜だ」のように，後ろから前に訳すのが基本だが，「〜こそ…する」などのように強調を表現して訳してもよい。

☑ condensed to cause ... の to cause ... は，**【結果】を表す不定詞の副詞用法**。

☑ **which は非制限用法の関係代名詞。先行詞は rainfall on the land**。

☑ **in turn は「今度は，同様に」の意味**。この熟語は以下の2つの関係を表す。ここでは①のタイプ(海水の蒸発→陸への降雨→塩分濃度上昇)。

　① A → B → C

　　例 The moon goes around the earth, and the earth, in turn, goes around the sun.
　　「月は地球の周りを回り，同様に地球は太陽の周りを回る」

　② A ⇄ B

　　例 I have always tried to help others in the belief that they would help me in turn someday.

　　　「私はいつも他人を助けようとしてきたが，それは，いつの日か，今度は
　　　彼らが私を助けてくれると信じてのことだ」

　※このほかに，in turn には「交代で，順々に」（＝by turns）の意味もある。

　　例 The president interviewed all the employees in turn.
　　　「社長は従業員全員と順々に面談を行った」

☑ 〈cause＋O＋to do〉は「（結果的に）Oに～させる」の意味。無生物主語構
　文で用いられるので，通常は「SのせいでOは～する」のように意訳する
　ほうが自然である。

問3

　下線部を含む文の直後の文に For instance「例えば」とあるので，この部分
をまとめればよい。なお，euryhaline「広塩性の」は受験生が知らないと思わ
れる語であるが，第2段落第1文（9 ～ 10行目）がこの語の説明になっているの
で，これを参考にして答案を作成すればよい。

問4

　まず，脊椎動物は，第4段落第1文（23 ～ 24行目）に列挙されている5種の
うち，**魚類とそれ以外（ほ乳類，鳥類，は虫類，両生類）で異なる進化をする**
ことが第6段落第2文（39行目）以降第7段落にかけて書かれており，この2つを
分けて答案を作る必要がある。**本問は「どのような要因」，「どのような進化」
と2つの内容が問われている**ことにも注意しよう。

　整理すると以下のようになるが，解答欄のスペースが限られており，全部は
書けないので，主要な内容をまとめるようにする。

	進化	要因，時代背景など
第6段落第1文（38 ～ 39行目）	脊椎動物が進化	海水の塩分濃度が今日の約4分の1
第6段落第2文（39 ～ 43行目）	脊椎動物のいくつかのグループ（鳥類，ほ乳類，は虫類，両生類）がさらに進化し，海を去り陸に住む	海水の塩分濃度が上昇 ↑ 〈蒸発⇒降雨⇒雨水に土壌のミネラル溶け込む⇒海へ戻る〉第3段落

第6段落 第3文 (43～45 行目)	陸上の脊椎動物は真水を飲み，食べ物から塩分を摂取することで血中塩分濃度を維持	
第7段落 第1文 (46行 目)	魚は水中環境にとどまる	
第7段落 第2文～ 最終文 (46～56 行目)	魚は腎臓の機能を変えたり，えらを発達させたりする	①淡水魚： 拡散により失われる塩分を取り戻し，過剰な水分を排出する必要性 ②海水魚： 浸透により失われる水分を取り戻し，過剰な塩分を排出する必要性

▼

それでは次に，段落ごとに詳しく見ていこう。 33
-
41

第1段落

¹The various species of fish found in oceans, lakes, rivers and streams have evolved over millions of years and have adapted to their preferred environments over long periods of time. ²Fish are categorized according to their salinity tolerance. ³Fish that can tolerate only very narrow ranges of salinity (such freshwater fish as goldfish and such saltwater fish as tuna) are known as stenohaline species. ⁴**These fish die in waters having a salinity that differs**
→ p.81 文構造Check!
from that in their natural environments.

訳 ¹海洋や湖，河川で見られるさまざまな種(しゅ)の魚は，何百万年もかけて進化してきたのであり，長期間にわたり自分の好む環境に適応してきた。²魚は塩分濃度に対する耐性に応じて分類される。³非常に狭い範囲の塩分濃度にしか耐性を持たない魚(金魚のような淡水魚やマグロのような海水魚)は狭塩性の種として知られている。⁴これらの魚は，自分たちの自然環境と異なる塩分濃度を有する水域では死んでしまう。

語句

species	名	(生物の)種
ocean	名	海, 海洋
stream	名	小川
evolve	動	進化する[させる], 発達する[させる]
adapt to ~	熟	~に適応する, ~に順応する
preferred	形	気に入った, 好ましい
environment	名	環境
categorize	動	分類する

according to ~	熟	~に応じて, ~に従って
salinity	名	塩分(濃度)
tolerance	名	耐性
tolerate	動	~に対しての耐性がある
range	名	範囲, 幅
freshwater	形	淡水の
goldfish	名	金魚
saltwater	形	海水の
tuna	名	マグロ
stenohaline	形	狭塩性の

文構造Check!

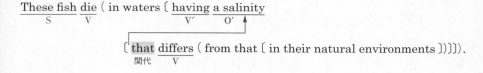

▶ having が現在分詞で, having 以下すべてが waters を修飾。salinity の後の that は主格の関係代名詞。from の後の that は the salinity を指す代名詞。

第2段落

[1]Fish that can tolerate a wide range of salinity at some phase in their life-cycle are called euryhaline species.　[2]These fish, which include salmon, eels, and striped bass, can live or survive in wide ranges of salinity, varying from fresh to brackish to marine waters. [3]**A period of gradual adjustment, though, may be needed for euryhaline fish to tolerate large changes in salinity.**

→ p.82　文構造Check!

> 訳　[1]ライフサイクルの中の一定時期に, 広い範囲の塩分濃度に耐え得る魚は, 広塩性の種と呼ばれる。[2]これらの魚は, それにはサケ, ウナギ, シマスズキが含まれるが, 淡水域から汽水域, 海水域に至るまで, さまざまな広い範囲の塩分濃度において生息し, あるいは生き残ることができるのである。[3]そうは言うものの, 広塩性の魚が塩分濃度の大きな変動に耐えるためには, 徐々に適応していく一定の期間が必要とされるかもしれない。

phase	名	段階，時期
life-cycle	名	(誕生から死までの)ライフサイクル，生涯過程
euryhaline	形	広塩性の
salmon	名	サケ
eel	名	ウナギ
striped bass	名	シマスズキ
survive	動	生き残る，生き延びる
vary	動	変化する，多様である
brackish	形	汽水性の，半塩水の
marine	形	海の
gradual	形	だんだんの，徐々の
adjustment	名	適応，順応
though	副	そうは言うものの，しかしながら

文構造Check!

A period of gradual adjustment, though, may be needed
               S   V

(for euryhaline fish to tolerate large changes 〔 in salinity 〕).
          S′   V′   O′

▶ though は「…けれど」の意味の従属接続詞の用法のほかに，副詞の用法がある。ここでは副詞の用法で，however と同様，文頭に but があるつもりで意味を取るとよい。for 以下は，〈for ... to *do*〉のパターンで，不定詞の意味上の主語を表している。「…が〜するために／〜するには」などと訳す。

第3段落

¹It is believed that when the newly formed planet Earth cooled sufficiently, rain began to fall continuously. ²This rainfall filled the first oceans with fresh water. ³It was the constant evaporation of water from the ocean that then condensed to cause rainfall on the land, which in turn, caused the ocean to become salty over several billion years. ⁴**As rain water washed over and through the soil,**
→ p.83　文構造Check!
it dissolved many minerals — sodium, potassium and calcium — and carried them back to the ocean.

訳 ¹新たに形成された地球という惑星が十分に冷却したとき，雨が連続的に降り始めたと考えられている。²この降雨が最初の海洋を淡水で満たした。³海からの絶え間ない水分の蒸発こそが，その後凝縮して陸に降雨をもたらし，今度はその降雨が原因で，海は何十億年にわたって塩分を多く含むようになった。⁴雨水は土壌の上や土壌の中を洗い流すとき，ナトリウム，カリウム，カルシウムといった多くのミネラルを溶かし，それらを運んで海に戻した。

語句

newly	副	新たに
form	動	形成する
sufficiently	副	十分に
continuously	副	連続的に，切れ目なく
rainfall	名	降雨
constant	形	絶え間ない，休みなく続く
evaporation	名	蒸発
condense	動	凝縮する，液化する

in turn	熟	今度は，同様に
salty	形	塩分を多く含む
wash	動	流れる，漂う
soil	名	土壌
dissolve	動	溶かす，溶解させる
mineral	名	ミネラル，鉱物
sodium	名	ナトリウム
calcium	名	カルシウム

文構造Check!

(As rain water washed (over and through the soil)),
従接　S　　　　　　V

it ⎰ dissolved many minerals — ⟨ sodium, potassium and calcium ⟩ —
S　　V①　　　　O

and
等接

carried them (back to the ocean).
V②　　O

▶ 文頭の接続詞 as は【時】を表す用法。wash(ed) は自動詞で「流れる」の意味。over and through the soil の部分は，前置詞 over と through が共に名詞 the soil をとる（共通関係）。over the soil は水が河川など土壌の上を流れること，through the soil は地下水など土壌の中を通って流れることを意味していると解される。

第4段落

[1]Vertebrate animals (fish, birds, mammals, reptiles and amphibians) have a unique and common characteristic. [2]The salt content of their blood is virtually identical. [3]Vertebrate blood has a salinity of approximately 9 grams per liter (a 0.9 percent salt solution). [4]Almost 77 percent of the salts in blood are sodium and chloride. [5]The remainder is made up primarily of bicarbonate, potassium and calcium. [6]Sodium, potassium and calcium salts are critical for the normal function of heart, nerve and muscle tissue.

> 訳 [1]脊椎動物(魚類, 鳥類, ほ乳類, は虫類, 両生類)は独特かつ共通の特徴を持っている。[2]それらの動物の血中塩分濃度はほぼ同じなのである。[3]脊椎動物の血液は1リットル当たり約9グラムの塩分濃度(0.9%の食塩水(塩類溶液))である。[4]血中塩分のほぼ77%はナトリウムと塩化物である。[5]残りは, 主に重炭酸塩, カリウム, カルシウムで構成される。[6]ナトリウム, カリウム, カルシウムの塩類は, 心臓, 神経, 筋肉の組織が正常に機能する上で重要なものである。

語句

mammal	名 ほ乳動物	**remainder**	名 残り
reptile	名 は虫類(の動物)	**be made up of ~**	熟 ~から成る, ~で構成される
amphibian	名 両生動物		
characteristic	名 特徴, 特色	**primarily**	副 主として
content	名 含有量	bicarbonate	名 重炭酸塩, 重曹
blood	名 血, 血液	**critical**	形 重大な
virtually	副 事実上, ほとんど	**normal**	形 正常な, 通常の
identical	形 同一の, 全く同じの	**function**	名 機能
approximately	副 およそ	**nerve**	名 神経
solution	名 溶液	**muscle**	名 筋肉
		tissue	名 組織

第5段落

[1]If the salinity of ocean water is diluted to approximately one quarter of its normal concentration, it has almost the same salinity as fish blood and contains similar proportions of sodium, potassium,

calcium and chloride. ²The similarities between the salt content of vertebrate blood and dilute seawater suggest a strong evolutionary relationship among vertebrates and with the ancient oceans.

訳 ¹仮に海水の塩分濃度を通常の濃度の約4分の1まで薄めると，魚の血液とほとんど同じ塩分濃度になり，ナトリウム，カリウム，カルシウム，塩化物が似たような比率で含まれることになる。²脊椎動物の血液と希釈した海水の塩分含有量が類似していることは，脊椎動物間の，および脊椎動物と大昔の海との進化上の強い関連性を示唆している。

語句

dilute	動 薄める，希釈する／形 薄めた，希釈した
concentration	名 濃度
contain	動 含む
proportion	名 割合，比率
similarity	名 類似(性)
suggest	動 示唆する，意味する
evolutionary	形 進化に関する，進化による

第6段落

¹Indeed, it seems likely that vertebrate life evolved when the ocean was approximately one quarter as salty as it is today. ²**As the ocean became saltier and vertebrates evolved further,** → p.86 文構造Check! **several groups of vertebrates (birds, mammals, reptiles and amphibians) left the ocean to inhabit the land, carrying the seawater with them as their blood.** ³They maintained their blood salt concentrations by drinking freshwater and absorbing salts from food.

訳 ¹実際，脊椎動物は海が今日の約4分の1の塩分濃度であったころに進化した可能性が高いようである。²海の塩分濃度が上がり，脊椎動物がさらに進化するにつれて，脊椎動物のいくつかのグループ(鳥類，ほ乳類，は虫類，両生類)は，海水を自らの血液として身につけながら，陸に住むために海を後にした。³そういった動物たちは真水を飲んだり食料から塩分を吸収したりすることで血中塩分濃度を維持した。

語句

indeed	副 実際に
further	副 さらに，それ以上に
inhabit	動 住む，居住する
maintain	動 維持する
absorb	動 吸収する

(As the ocean became saltier and vertebrates evolved further),
　従接　S　　　 V　　　 C　　等接　　 S　　　　 V

　　　several groups of vertebrates (birds, mammals, reptiles and amphibians)
　　　　　　　　 S

　　　left the ocean (to inhabit the land),
　　　 V　　 O

　　　　　　　　(carrying the seawater (with them) (as their blood)).
　　　　　　　　　 V′　　　 O′

▶ 文頭の As は【比例】を表す接続詞で，「…するにつれて」の意味。carrying ... は【付帯状況】を表す分詞構文。

第7段落

¹But fish stayed in the aquatic environment. ²To adapt, they had to either remain in low salinity environments, such as bays and estuaries, or they had to evolve mechanisms to replace water lost through osmosis to the seawater and to remove salts absorbed from the increasingly saline oceans. ³To inhabit fresh water, fish had to replace salts lost through diffusion to the water and eliminate excess water absorbed from the environment. ⁴Kidney function had to be altered accordingly for fish to survive in these different habitats. ⁵Eventually, the gills developed the ability to excrete salts in seawater and absorb salts from fresh water.

訳 ¹しかし，魚類は水中環境にとどまった。²順応するために，魚は入り江や河口といった塩分濃度の低い環境にとどまるか，海水への浸透により失われる水を補ったり，ますます塩分を多く含むようになった海から吸収した塩分を取り除いたりする仕組みを発達させる必要があった。³淡水に住むためには，水への拡散により失われる塩分を取り戻し，周囲から吸収した余分な水を排泄(せつ)しなければならなかった。⁴魚がこれらの異なる生息場所で生き延びるために，それに応じて腎臓の機能は変えられなければならなかった。⁵最終的に，えらが海水中に塩分を排出し，淡水から塩分を吸収する能力を発達させた。

語句

aquatic	形	水中の，水生の
bay	名	湾，入り江
mechanism	名	仕組み，構造
replace	動	元に戻す，補う
remove	動	取り除く，除去する
saline	形	塩分を含んだ
eliminate	動	排泄する，排除する

excess	形	余分な，過度の
environment	名	環境，周囲
kidney	名	腎臓
alter	動	変える
accordingly	副	それにしたがって，そのように
habitat	名	生息地
eventually	副	結局，最終的に

第8段落

¹In seawater, fish must drink salt water to replace lost fluids and then eliminate the excess salts. ²Their kidneys produce small volumes of fluid containing high concentrations of salt. ³Freshwater fish produce large volumes of dilute urine, which is low in salt. ⁴High concentrations of environmental calcium help reduce salt loss through the gills and body surfaces in freshwater environments. ⁵Less demand is placed on the kidneys to maintain stable concentrations of blood salts in brackish or low salinity waters.

訳 ¹海水中で魚は失われた体液を取り戻すために塩水を飲み，その後余分な塩分を排泄しなければならない。²魚の腎臓は高濃度の塩分を含む少量の分泌液を作り出す。³淡水魚は多量の希釈尿を作り出すが，これは塩分が少ない。⁴周囲にある高濃度のカルシウムが，淡水の環境下における，えらや体表からの塩分喪失を減らすのに役立つ。⁵汽水や塩分濃度の低い水域においては，一定の血中塩分濃度を維持するために，腎臓にそれほど多くの要求がなされるわけではない。

語句

fluid	名	体液，分泌液
produce	動	産出する，作り出す
volume	名	量
urine	名	尿
environmental	形	環境の，周囲の

reduce	動	減らす
surface	名	表面
demand	名	要求
▶ **place a demand on ～**		～に要求を押しつける
stable	形	安定した

第9段落

[1]Ultimately, fish adapted to or inhabited marine, fresh or brackish water because each environment offered some competitive advantage to the different species. [2]For instance, it has been suggested that euryhaline fish are able to eliminate external parasites by moving to and from fresh and saltwaters. [3]Habitats of wide ranges of salinity offered new or more food, escape from predators and even stable temperatures.

> **訳** [1]最終的に，魚類は海水，淡水，汽水のいずれかに順応したり住みついたりした。それは，それぞれの環境が異なる種に対して何らかの競争上の利益を与えたからだ。[2]例えば，広塩性の魚は，淡水と海水を行き来することで外部の寄生虫を排除することができることが示唆されてきた。[3]塩分濃度が広範囲にわたる生息場所は新しいえさや豊富なえさ，捕食者からの逃避手段，さらには安定した水温を提供してくれた。

語句

ultimately	副	最終的に，結局
offer	動	提供する，与える
competitive	形	競争（上）の
advantage	名	有利，利益
external	形	外部の

parasite	名	寄生虫
to and from ～	熟	～を行き来して
escape	名	逃避（手段）
predator	名	捕食者，捕食動物
temperature	名	温度

88

パラグラフ展開　　英文全体の内容を把握しよう！

主題　魚と塩分濃度

第1段落

魚は長い年月をかけて環境に適応

➡ 魚の分類：salinity tolerance「塩分濃度に対する耐性」による

　① stenohaline species「狭塩性の種」：海水魚，淡水魚

第2段落

　② euryhaline species「広塩性の種」：汽水魚

前提事実の整理

第3段落

新しくできた地球が冷却した

・降雨により海が淡水で満たされる

・海から蒸発した水が降雨になる

・土壌のミネラル分を雨水が海に運ぶ

・海の塩分濃度が上昇

第4段落

脊椎動物（魚類，鳥類，ほ乳類，は虫類，両生類）＝血液中の塩分濃度がほぼ等しい

第5段落

海水を約4分の1に希釈すると魚の血液と濃度も成分比もほぼ等しくなる

第6段落

①脊椎動物は海水の塩分濃度が現在の約4分の1のころに進化

②塩分濃度上昇に伴い，鳥類・ほ乳類・は虫類・両生類は陸へ

➡ 海水を血液として身につける

➡ 真水を飲んだり，食べ物から塩分をとったりして，塩分濃度を維持

第7段落

③魚類は水中にとどまる

➡ 塩分濃度が上昇する海に適応するために…

(1)塩分濃度の低い場所(入り江や河口)に住む

(2)海水では水分を取り戻し，塩分を排出する仕組み

(3)淡水では水分を排出し，塩分を取り戻す仕組み

第8段落

③の(2)(3)についての具体化

補足

第9段落

海水魚，淡水魚，汽水魚がそれぞれに有利な環境に生育

テーマ解説

　脊椎動物の進化の過程で，魚類がほかの脊椎動物と違う道を歩む経緯を，生物の体液と海水の濃度や組成との関係から解き明かすという，専門性の高い英文。生物の進化は記録が残っているわけではないので，残されている数少ない手がかりから解明しなくてはならないが，謎が解き明かされるプロセスは興味深い。本問と似たタイプの英文としては，かつて防衛医科大学校(医学科)の長文問題(2008年)で，身体の各部位に寄生するシラミの種類から，類人猿の進化の過程が解明されるという内容の英文が出題されたことがある。こういった専門性の高い文は時系列の展開，要因を示す説明が続くなど，やや複雑になるので，英文を読みながらメモを取って整理すると内容が理解しやすくなる。

確認問題

/40点

1. ①〜⑩は語句の意味を日本語で書き、⑪〜⑳は和訳と対応する英語の語句を、頭文字を参考にして書き、空欄を完成させよう。（各1点×20）

① tolerance 名 _____

② range 名 _____

③ evaporation 名 _____

④ mammal 名 _____

⑤ nerve 名 _____

⑥ proportion 名 _____

⑦ eliminate 動 _____

⑧ excess 形 _____

⑨ stable 形 _____

⑩ competitive 形 _____

⑪ s _____ 名 （生物の）種

⑫ a _____ t ～ 熟 ～に適応する、～に順応する

⑬ p _____ 名 段階、時期

⑭ s _____ 動 生き残る、生き延びる

⑮ v _____ 動 変化する、多様である

⑯ d _____ 動 溶かす、溶解させる

⑰ i _____ 動 住む、居住する

⑱ a _____ 動 吸収する

⑲ a _____ 動 変える

⑳ a _____ 名 有利、利益

2. 次の[ ]の語句を並べ替えて、意味の通る英文を完成させよう。（各5点×2）

① These fish [differs / in / waters / die / from / having / a salinity / that] that in their natural environments.

これらの魚は，自分たちの自然環境と異なる塩分濃度を有する水域では死んでしまう。

② Indeed, it seems likely that vertebrate life evolved when the ocean [is /
salty / approximately / was / one / quarter / as / as / it] today.

実際，脊椎動物は海が今日の約4文の1の塩分濃度であったころに進化した可能性が高いようで
ある。

3. 次の英文を和訳してみよう。(10点)

A period of gradual adjustment, though, may be needed for euryhaline
fish to tolerate large changes in salinity.

ディクテーションしてみよう！

今回学習した英文に出てきた語句を，音声を聞いて＿＿＿＿に書き取ろう。

42　　The various species of fish found in oceans, lakes, rivers and streams
❶＿＿＿＿＿＿＿＿＿＿＿＿＿＿＿＿＿ and have adapted to their preferred
environments over long periods of time.　Fish are categorized according to
their salinity tolerance.　Fish that ❷＿＿＿＿＿＿＿＿＿＿＿＿＿＿＿＿＿＿
salinity (such freshwater fish as goldfish and such saltwater fish as tuna)
are known as stenohaline species.　These fish die in waters having a salinity
that differs from that in their natural environments.

43　　Fish that can tolerate a wide range of salinity ❸＿＿＿＿＿＿＿
＿＿＿＿＿＿ are called euryhaline species.　These fish, which include
salmon, eels, and striped bass, can live or survive in wide ranges of salinity,
varying from fresh to brackish to marine waters.　❹＿＿＿＿＿＿＿＿＿＿
＿＿＿＿, though, may be needed for euryhaline fish to tolerate large
changes in salinity.

確認問題の答

1. ①耐性　　②範囲，幅　　③蒸発　　④ほ乳動物　　⑤神経　　⑥割合，比率
　　⑦排泄する，排除する　　⑧余分な，過度の　　⑨安定した　　⑩競争(上)の　　⑪ species
　　⑫ adapt to　　⑬ phase　　⑭ survive　　⑮ vary　　⑯ dissolve　　⑰ inhabit　　⑱ absorb
　　⑲ alter　　⑳ advantage
2. ① die in waters having a salinity that differs from　（第1段落　最終文）
　　② was approximately one quarter as salty as it is　（第6段落　第1文）
3. そうは言うものの，広塩性の魚が塩分濃度の大きな変動に耐えるためには，徐々に適応していく一定の期間
　　が必要とされるかもしれない。　（第2段落　最終文）

ディクテーションしてみよう！の答

　　❶ have evolved over millions of years
　　❷ can tolerate only very narrow ranges of　　❸ at some phase in their life-cycle
　　❹ A period of gradual adjustment

解 答

問1	全訳参照
問2	do your research
問3	ホテルの環境保護に関する認証の正当性を調査し，旅行代理店に連絡して環境保護への取り組みについての細かい質問をし，ホテルのウェブサイトも詳しく調べること。**(76字)**
問4	**(A)** ③ **(B)** ④ **(C)** ④

解 説

問1

　文構造を確認しよう。

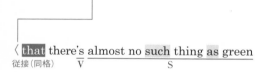

イディオム
(When it comes to airlines and cruise ship companies,)
等接

there's a consensus (among experts)
　　V　　　　S

〈 that there's almost no such thing as green
従接(同格)　V　　　　　　　S

— only shades of fake green. 〉

以下のポイントをおさえよう！

☑ when it comes to ~「~のことになると，~について言えば」

☑ airlines と cruise ship companies が and により並列されている。

☑ that は同格の接続詞で，consensus の具体的内容を示す。同格の that と説明される名詞が離れている点に注意。

☑ such A as B「Bのような A」

☑ shade には「陰」の他に，可算名詞で「色合い，色調」の意味がある。

☑ — only shades of fake green の部分は，直前の there's almost no such thing as green を補足する働き。only の前に there are を補って考えるとよい。

問2

> You need to (2)"dig deep" on a hotel's website to determine ...
> …を判断するためには，ホテルのウェブサイトを＿＿＿＿＿する必要がある。

　dig deep を直訳すれば「深く掘り下げる」。ウェブサイト上で深く掘り下げるというのは，細かいところまで見るという意味だと推測できる。

◆第3段落第1文
> An eco-travel specialist advises travelers to do your research to determine whether green travel options are legitimate.

　直後の to determine が共通しているので，この箇所を見つけることは難しくないだろう。正解は do your research「調査する」となる。

　なお，形が似ているものとしては，第3段落第3文（But if you travel abroad, you'll need to be aware of other sustainability-certification programs, ...）の be aware of も考えられる（直前の need to が共通）。ただ，意味もかなり異なる上に，be aware of は前置詞 of の後に名詞を必要とするので，下線部分と置き換えられない。

問3

> Perhaps the best travelers can hope for is that (3)their preference for sustainability will make the industry more responsive to their concerns.

　下線部の内容は，make が第5文型（S+V+O+C）で「OをCにする」の意味で用いられていることに注目し（⇒ 106 ページ　文構造 CHECK! 参照），以下のように理解する。

＜直訳＞
　旅行者が持続可能性を好むことが旅行産業をそのような関心にもっと対応するようにさせる
　　↓
＜意訳＞
　旅行者が持続可能性を好むことにより旅行産業がそのような関心に対してもっと対応してくれるようになる

設問の「消費者」とは，旅行産業の消費者，つまり旅行者を意味している。そこで，旅行者が持続可能性を好むことを示すような行動を本文から抽出すればよい。以下の4カ所がこれに該当する。

❶第3段落第1文

An eco-travel specialist advises travelers to <u>do your research to determine whether green travel options are legitimate</u>.

❷第5段落第3・4文

The best advice is to <u>contact your travel agent and ask some detailed questions</u>. Those include: What hotels do you prefer to send your travelers to and why? What common travel practices do you see that you don't like? How do you operate in a more eco-friendly way?

❸第6段落第2文

You'd better see where they are obtaining their food, what they do with leftovers, and what cleaning products they use.

❹第7段落第1文

You need to <u>"dig deep" on a hotel's website</u> to determine things such as the materials used to create the building, its efforts to save fuel and water, and green certifications.

これらすべてを書くのは字数制限の観点から無理なので，具体的な質問やチェックの内容をカットすると，波線で示した部分になるだろう（❸は具体的なチェック項目のみなので全てカット）。❶については，ここだけでは green travel options の意味が不明確だが，同段落第2文以降を読めば，ホテルの環境配慮に関する certification（認証）のことだとわかるので，そのように書くとよい。

整理すると以下のような答案になるだろう。

❶⇒ホテルの環境保護に関する認証の正当性を調査し，

❷⇒旅行代理店に連絡して環境保護への取り組みについての細かい質問をし，

❹⇒ホテルのウェブサイトも詳しく調べること。

問4

(A) And then people would let nature take its (　　　　).

take *one's* course は「コース［進路］を進む」，つまり，「自然の経過をた
どる，なりゆきのままに進む」の意味。使役動詞 let「〜させる，〜させ
ておく」と組み合わせた let 〜 take *one's* course は，「〜にそのコース
を進ませる」，つまり，「〜をなりゆきに任せる」の意味。

内容面を確認すると，環境保護の観点で理想の状態があるとしたら，ホ
テルは取り壊し，そこに木を植えることになると書かれているので，人
工的なものを排除して自然のありのままの姿にするという意味にすれば
文脈にも合う。

(B) If you don't like the answers or if they seem (　　　　), go elsewhere.

環境に配慮したホテルを見極める方法について助言している文脈。環境
保護への取り組みについて質問し，「もし回答が気に入らないか，＿＿＿
と感じた場合は，他の場所［ホテル］に行きなさい」とあるので，否定的
な内容が入るはず。この時点で②「魅力的な」，③「説得力のある」は
除外できる。①の engaged は多義語で，「婚約して」「携わって，従事し
て」「忙しい」「使用中で」などの意味を持つが，いずれも質問への回答
を形容するのに適さない。④の suspicious は「疑わしい，不審な」の意
味で，ホテル側からの回答が本当に環境に配慮しているのか疑わしい，
と解釈すれば意味が通る。

(C) No travel agency will come up (　　　　).

直後の文（After all, every airplane, cruise ship, hotel, and resort pollutes
the environment.）の内容から，旅行代理店がどのような旅行プランを提
供しても環境破壊をゼロにはできないと考えられる。come up は直後に
補語を取り，「結局〜になる」の意味。「どんな旅行代理店も完璧にはな
らない」とすれば意味が通る。正解は④「完璧な」。他の選択肢の意味
は，①「不在の」②「遠方の」③「全体の」。

第1段落

¹Green may not be the most fashionable color this spring, but it's still popular among many travelers. ²A survey found that 58 percent of hotel guests preferred staying at an environmentally friendly property. ³Nearly 40 percent said they're willing to spend an extra $10 a night to sleep at a sustainable resort. **⁴If you're a hotel** → p.99　文構造Check! **manager, hanging a sign on your door that says you're green — even if you aren't — can increase profits**. ⁵A study found that 60 percent of U.S. travelers have taken a "sustainable" trip in the last three years and that these travelers spend on average $600 per trip, and stay three days longer than the average guest. ⁶The expanding green-travel market is now "too big to ignore."

> 訳 ¹グリーンはこの春，最も流行している色ではないかもしれないが，多くの旅行者の間で依然として人気がある。²ある調査によれば，ホテル宿泊客の58％が環境に配慮した施設に宿泊することを好むということがわかった。³40％近くの人が持続可能なリゾートで1泊につき10ドル余分に支払うことをいとわないと述べている。⁴もしホテルのマネージャーであれば，（たとえ実際はそうでなくても）グリーンである[環境に優しい]という看板をドアに掲げることで利益を増やすことができるだろう。⁵ある研究によると，アメリカの旅行者の60％が過去3年間に「持続可能な」旅行を経験し，これらの旅行者は平均して1回の旅行に600ドルを費やし，通常の宿泊客よりも3日間長く滞在していることがわかっている。⁶拡大するグリーン旅行[環境に優しい旅行]市場は今や「無視できないほど大きい」ものとなっている。

語句

fashionable 形 流行している	**be willing to *do*** 熟 ～することをいとわない，進んで～する
property 名 不動産，土地，建物	
sustainable 形 持続可能な	**expand** 動 拡大する

文構造Check!

(**If** you're a hotel manager,)
従接 S　V　　　　C

従接 that 省略

green 省略

〈 hanging a sign on your door 〔 **that** says 〈 you're green〉〕— (even if you aren't)—〉
S　　　　　　　　　　　V　　O

関代

can increase profits.
V　　　　　　O

▶ that は主格の関係代名詞で，先行詞は a sign。

第2段落

¹Yet some travelers remain unsure about green travel.　²"For me, green implies no manufactured products," says a frequent traveler. ³And by that standard, no airplane, cruise ship, or hotel can truly be considered green.　**⁴In a perfect world, for a hotel to be considered green, it would have to be completely demolished, and trees would have to be planted over it.**　⁵And then people would let nature take its course.　⁶But that's not the world we live in. ⁷Still, at a time when terms like "green," "sustainable," and "environmentally friendly" are used too much — often with the intent of convincing you to make a travel plan — it's worth asking how to separate real green from fake green.

→ p.100　文構造Check!

訳 ¹しかし，一部の旅行者はグリーン旅行についてまだ疑念を抱いている。²「私にとって，グリーンとは，既製品を一切含まないことを意味します」と，頻繁に旅行する人は言う。³そして，その基準に従えば，いかなる飛行機も，クルーズ船も，ホテルも，本当にグリーンであるとは考えられない。⁴仮に理想の世界であるとしたら，ホテルがグリーンであるとみなされるためには，完全に解体されてその上に木が植えられなければならないだろう。⁵そして，人々はその後，自然をなりゆきに任せることになるだろう。⁶しかし，私たちが生きているのはそのような世界ではない。⁷それでも，「グリーン」「持続可能な」「環境に優しい」といった言葉が，多くの場合旅行計画を立てるよう説得する意図で，あまりにも多用されている時代においては，本物のグリーンと偽物のグリーンをどう区別するかを問うことは価値がある。

文構造 Check!

(In a perfect world,)

(for a hotel to be considered green,)
　　S'　　　　　V'　　　　C'

it would have to be completely demolished, and trees would have to be planted
S　　　　　　　V　　　　　　　　　　　　　等接　S　　　　　　V

(over it).

▶ In a perfect world は仮定法の if 節の代用。「仮に理想の[完全な]世界であれば」の意味。仮定法なので主節では助動詞 would が用いられている。for a hotel to be ... の部分は，for が不定詞の意味上の主語を表しており，「…が〜するために」の意味。

第3段落

[1]An eco-travel specialist advises travelers to do your research to determine whether green travel options are legitimate. [2]For example, many hotels promote their Leadership in Energy and Environmental Design (LEED) certification from the U.S. Green Building Council, which judges on criteria such as water savings, energy efficiency, and building material selection. [3]But if you travel abroad, you'll need to be aware of other sustainability-certification programs, such as Australia's EarthCheck or Britain's Green

Tourism Business Scheme. ⁴Hotel chains sometimes have their own sustainability standards. ⁵InterContinental Hotels Group, which owns the Holiday Inn and Crowne Plaza brands, runs an internal program called "IHG Green Engage" that lets its hotels measure their environmental impact. ⁶Owners can view reports on water use and utility consumption with an eye toward reducing their carbon and water waste.

訳 ¹エコ旅行[環境に優しい旅行]の専門家は，旅行者に対して，グリーン旅行のオプションが正当なものかどうかを判断するために調査するよう助言する。²例えば，多くのホテルがアメリカのグリーンビルディング評議会からの「Leadership in Energy and Environmental Design(LEED)」認証を推進しており，これは，節水，エネルギー効率，建築資材の選択などの基準で評価を行うものである。³しかし，海外に旅行する場合は，オーストラリアの EarthCheck やイギリスの Green Tourism Business Scheme などの他の持続可能性認証プログラムも意識する必要がある。⁴ホテルチェーンには独自の持続可能性基準を持っているものもある。⁵ホリデイ・インやクラウンプラザを所有するインターコンチネンタルホテルグループは，「IHG Green Engage」という，ホテルが環境への影響を測定することができる内部プログラムを運営している。⁶オーナーは炭素排出と水の浪費を削減することに注目しつつ，水の使用量や公共サービス消費に関する報告書を見ることができる。

語句

legitimate	形 正当な，本物の	material	名 材料，資材
promote	動 促進する，推進する	internal	形 (組織)内部の
certification	名 証明書，認証	utility	名 公共サービス(ガス，水道，電気など)，公共料金
criterion	名 基準，尺度		
	*複数形：criteria	with an eye toward ~	
saving	名 節約		熟 ~に目を向けて，~を見据えて
efficiency	名 効率，能率	carbon	名 炭素

第4段落

¹When it comes to airlines and cruise ship companies, there's a consensus among experts that there's almost no such thing as green — only shades of fake green. ²It's said that there's a lot of greenwashing and both airplanes and cruise ship companies pollute

to such an extent that some travelers find it difficult to justify a reservation.

訳 ¹航空会社やクルーズ船会社については，専門家の間では，グリーン[環境への配慮]といったものはほとんどなく，偽物のグリーンの色合いのみが存在するという一致した見解がある。²環境に配慮した姿勢を装うことが横行しており，飛行機もクルーズ船会社も汚染を大いに引き起こしているため，旅行の予約をするのを正当化しにくくなっている旅行者もいると言われる。

語句

when it comes to ~ 熟 ~のことになると，
                      ~について言えば
airline   名 航空会社
consensus   名 合意，意見の一致
shade   名 色合い，色調

extent   名 程度，度合い
▶~ to such an extent that ...
    相当な程度に~なので…
justify   動 正当化する
reservation   名 予約

第 5 段落

¹It can be even more difficult to assess tours that combine air travel, hotel stays, and sightseeing into a single package because of their many components. ²It's not always easy to tell apart authentic green, eco-friendly, and sustainable tours from fakes. ³The best advice is to contact your travel agent and ask some detailed questions. ⁴Those include: What hotels do you prefer to send your travelers to and why? ⁵What common travel practices do you see that you don't like? ⁶How do you operate in a more eco-friendly way? ⁷By making a little bit of extra effort and asking the right questions, you can increase the likelihood that you are dealing with someone who shares your values.

訳 ¹飛行機による旅行，ホテル滞在，観光を１つのパッケージに組み合わせたツアーを評価することは，多くの構成要素からなるため，さらに困難となりうる。²本物のグリーンで環境に優しく持続可能なツアーを偽物と区別することは必ずしも容易ではない。³最良のアドバイスは，旅行代理店に連絡して詳細な質問をすることだ。⁴そういった質問に含まれるのは，以下のようなものである。旅行者をどのホテルに送り届けたいと思うか，またそれはなぜか。⁵よくある好ましくない旅行の習慣で，あなたが目にするのはどのようなものか。⁶どのようにしてより環境に優しい方法で営業しているのか。⁷少し余分な努力をして適切な質問をすることで，自分の価値観を共有する人と取引する可能性を高めることができる。

語句

assess	動	評価する，査定する
combine	動	結びつける，組み合わせる
▶ **combine _A_ into _B_**		_A_ を組み合わせて B にする
sightseeing	名	観光
component	名	(構成)要素
tell apart	熟	区別する
authentic	形	本物の，真正の
eco-friendly	形	環境に優しい，環境を破壊しない
travel agent	名	旅行代理店
detailed	形	詳細な，細かい
operate	動	営業する，運営する
extra	形	追加の，余分の
likelihood	名	可能性
deal with ~	熟	~と取引する

第 6 段落

¹Aside from what light bulbs they use, how many recycling boxes you see, or whether they give you the option to decline daily room service, it's hard to tell at first sight how sustainable a hotel is really trying to be. ²You'd better see where they are obtaining their food, what they do with leftovers, and what cleaning products they use. ³If you don't like the answers or if they seem suspicious, go elsewhere. ⁴Simply stating that they are green or eco-friendly does not guarantee that they are not greenwashing.

¹いかなる電球を使用しているか，リサイクルボックスがいくつ目に入るか，または毎日のルームサービスを辞退するオプションを与えてくれるかどうかといったことを除けば，実際にどの程度持続可能なホテルであろうと務めているかを一目で見極めるのは困難だ。²食品をどこで入手しているか，残り物をどのように処理しているか，いかなる洗剤を用いているかを確認した方がよいだろう。³もし回答が気に入らないか，疑わしいと感じた場合は，他の場所に行きなさい。⁴ただ自らがグリーンであるとか環境に優しいと言っているだけでは，環境への配慮が偽りでないという保証にはならない。

語句

aside from ～	熟	～以外に，～を除けば	**obtain** 動 得る，手に入れる
light bulb	名	電球	**leftover** 名 (料理の)残り物
decline	動	断る，辞退する	**cleaning product** 名 洗剤，洗浄剤
at first sight	熟	一目で，見た途端に	**suspicious** 形 疑わしい
			guarantee 動 保証する

第7段落

¹You need to "dig deep" on a hotel's website to determine things such as the materials used to create the building, its efforts to save fuel and water, and green certifications. ²If that information is missing, perhaps the hotel's commitment to sustainability just isn't there.

¹建物を作るのに使われた材料，燃料と水を節約する取り組み，グリーンの認証などの事柄を判断するためには，ホテルのウェブサイトを「詳細に調べる」必要がある。² その情報が欠けている場合，おそらくそのホテルの持続可能性への取り組みは全く存在しないのだろう。

語句

dig deep	熟	詳しく調べる	**missing** 形 ない，欠けている
fuel	名	燃料	**commitment** 名 取り組み，関わり

第8段落

¹No travel agency will come up perfect. ²After all, every airplane, cruise ship, hotel, and resort pollutes the environment. ³**Perhaps**
→ p.105 文構造Check!
the best travelers can hope for is that their preference for

sustainability will make the industry more responsive to their concerns. ⁴Because, in the end, the only thing the travel industry probably cares about is your money.

> **訳** ¹完璧な旅行代理店は今後も出てこないだろう。²結局のところ，飛行機，クルーズ船，ホテル，リゾートはすべて環境を汚染しているのだ。³おそらく，旅行者が望みうることは，せいぜい，自分が持続可能性を好むことにより旅行産業がそのような関心に対してもっと対応してくれるようになることぐらいだろう。⁴なぜなら，最終的には，旅行産業がおそらく気にかけているのは客の金だけだからだ。

語句

come up ~	熟 結局~になる，~な状態で現れる	responsive	形 反応して，応じて
sustainability	名 持続可能性	concern	名 関心事
		care about ~	熟 ~を気にする

文構造Check!

関代 that 省略

Perhaps the best 〔 travelers can hope for 〕
　　　　 S 　　　　 S 　　　 V

is 〈 that their preference for sustainability will make the industry
V C 従接 　　　　　 S 　　　　　　　　　 V 　　　 O

　　　　　　　　　　　　 more responsive to their concerns. 〉
　　　　　　　　　　　　　　　　　 C

▶ the best が S で，その後に関係代名詞の節が続く。best は「最もよいもの，最善のもの」の意味の名詞。hope for の後に目的語がないことから，関係代名詞 that の目的格の省略を見抜く。the best travelers ... を見て「最善の旅行者は…」などと誤訳しないように。

第1段落 主題の提示

グリーン（＝ 環境に優しい）旅行が人気

第2段落 問題提起

グリーン旅行への疑念

⇒本物のグリーンと偽物のグリーンの見分けは？

＜具体的な見分け方＞

第3段落 認証プログラムによってグリーンかどうか見分ける

第4段落 飛行機やクルーズ船 ＝ グリーンはほぼゼロ

第5段落 パックツアー ＝ 構成要素が多く判断難しい

⇒旅行代理店に質問

第6段落 ホテルがグリーンかどうかの判断

⇒食品，洗剤などをチェック

※自称グリーンは偽物かも

第7段落 ホテルのウェブサイトを詳しく調べる

⇒建材，燃料，水の節約，etc.

第8段落 結論

旅行産業は全て環境を汚染

⇒ 持続可能性への旅行者の関心に対応することを期待するのみ

∵旅行産業は金儲けしか考えていない

テーマ解説

　観光産業は多くの国々にとって重要な産業である。我が国も観光産業が国内総生産（GDP）に大きく寄与しており，直接・間接的に多くの雇用を創出している。外貨獲得手段としても，地域振興にとっても，観光産業は重要な役割を果たす。他方で，いわゆるオーバーツーリズム（overtourism；過剰な観光客の来訪）などにより，環境への悪影響が懸念されており，これを解決するために，環境に配慮した旅行（green travel）が試みられている。

環境に優しい旅行（eco-friendly travel）をするために考慮すべき点を挙げよう。
①交通手段の選択
　飛行機の利用が増加することで，CO_2 排出量が増加する懸念がある。航空業界は環境に配慮した技術開発やエネルギー効率の向上を進めているが，まだ課題が残っている。地域内での公共交通機関や自転車，徒歩の利用を奨励することがエコ旅行の一環として考えられるが，インフラやアクセスの制約がある。
②宿泊施設の選択
　宿泊施設の選択において，環境に配慮した宿泊施設を選択すべきである。エネルギー効率のよい施設や廃棄物の適切な処理を行う施設を選ぶことが求められる。本文第３段落でも言及されていた，旅行産業における認証制度やプログラム（米国の LEED，オーストラリアの EarthCheck，英国の Green Tourism Business Scheme，インターコンチネンタルグループの IHG Green Engage）も参考になる。
③観光地の持続可能性
　観光客の過剰な増加（overtourism）による自然環境への影響や，文化財への負担が懸念される。
④地域社会への影響
　観光が地域経済に貢献する一方で，地域の資源消費や物価上昇，土地利用の変化など，地域社会への潜在的な影響が懸念される。一部の地域では観光需要に合わせて短期間で賃金や物価が高騰し，観光以外の地元企業や地域住民に悪影響が及んでいる。
⑤偽善的な環境への配慮（greenwashing）
　一部の企業や施設が green ／ sustainable ／ eco-friendly といったキャッチフレーズで環境に優しいイメージを装っているが，実際には環境に対する取り組みがほとんどなされていない場合がある。これを greenwashing（本文第４段落参照）と呼び，消費者を欺く可能性がある。

確認問題

1. ①～⑩は語句の意味を日本語で書き，⑪～⑳は和訳と対応する英語の語句を，頭文字を参考にして書き，空欄を完成させよう。（各1点×20）

/40点

① manufacture	動		
② demolish	動		
③ certification	名		
④ criterion	名		
⑤ consensus	名		
⑥ sightseeing	名		
⑦ authentic	形		
⑧ aside from ～	熟		
⑨ leftover	名		
⑩ suspicious	形		
⑪ i	動	暗示する	
⑫ e	名	効率，能率	
⑬ a	動	評価する，査定する	
⑭ c	名	(構成)要素	
⑮ l ___ b	名	電球	
⑯ d	動	断る，辞退する	
⑰ o	動	得る，手に入れる	
⑱ g	動	保証する	
⑲ f	名	燃料	
⑳ m	形	ない，欠けている	

2. 次の[　]の語句を並べ替えて，意味の通る英文を完成させよう。（各5点×2）

① It's said that there's a lot of greenwashing and both airplanes and cruise ship companies pollute [to / find / that / an extent / such / it / travelers / some / difficult] to justify a reservation.

108

環境に配慮した姿勢を装うことが横行しており，飛行機もクルーズ船会社も汚染を大いに引き起こしているため，旅行の予約をするのを正当化しにくくなっている旅行者もいると言われる。

② By making a little bit of extra effort and asking the right questions, you can increase the [shares / with / likelihood / someone / that / are / dealing / you / your / who / values].

少し余分な努力をして適切な質問をすることで，自分の価値観を共有する人と取引する可能性を高めることができる。

3. 次の英文を和訳してみよう。(10 点)

Perhaps the best travelers can hope for is that their preference for sustainability will make the industry more responsive to their concerns.

ディクテーションしてみよう！

今回学習した英文に出てきた語句を，音声を聞いて＿＿＿＿に書き取ろう。

52　Green may not be the most fashionable color this spring, but it's still popular among many travelers.　A survey found that 58 percent of hotel guests preferred staying ❶＿＿＿＿＿＿＿＿＿＿＿＿＿＿＿＿.　Nearly 40 percent said they're willing to spend an extra $10 a night to sleep at a sustainable resort.　If you're a hotel manager, hanging a sign on your door that says you're green — even if you aren't — can increase profits.　A study found that 60 percent of U.S. travelers have taken a "sustainable" trip in the last three years and that ❷＿＿＿＿＿＿＿＿＿＿＿＿＿＿＿＿＿＿, and stay three days longer than the average guest.　The expanding green-travel market is now "too big to ignore."

53　Yet some travelers remain unsure about green travel.　"For me, green implies no manufactured products," says a frequent traveler.　And by that standard, no airplane, cruise ship, or hotel can truly be considered green.　In a perfect world, ❸＿＿＿＿＿＿＿＿＿＿＿＿＿＿＿, it would have

to be completely demolished, and trees would have to be planted over it. And then people would let nature take its course. But that's not the world we live in. Still, at a time when terms like "green," "sustainable," and "environmentally friendly" are used too much — often with the intent of convincing you to make a travel plan — ❹_____
_____.

解 答

問1 頭を悩ませながら論理問題を解いているときに，一定のパターンで目を動かすよう求められたグループの人々は，問題を解ける可能性が２倍高かった。

問2 this new model of mind

問3 脳の中で起こっていることは，身体全体で起こっていること，およびその身体が環境の中でどのように位置づけられているか，によって主として決定されるかもしれないのである。

問4 もし我々が直立歩行していないなら，あるいは恒温動物でないなら，これらの概念を全く違ったふうに理解するかもしれない。

問5 人間は実際には，コンピュータがするように形式的なルールを用い抽象的な記号を操作することで情報を処理しているのではない。

問6 ⑥

解 説

問1

$\underset{\text{S}}{\underline{\text{a group of people}}}$

〔 asked to move their eyes (in a specific pattern)

（ while $\underset{\text{従接}}{\text{while}}$ $\underset{\text{V}}{\underline{\text{puzzling through}}}$ $\underset{\text{O}}{\underline{\text{a logical problem}}}$ ）〕

（they were 省略 $\underset{\text{S \ (V)}}{}$）

$\underset{\text{V}}{\underline{\text{were twice as likely to solve}}}$ $\underset{\text{O}}{\underline{\text{it}}}$

以下のポイントをおさえよう！

☑ asked は過去形ではなく過去分詞形。〈**ask＋O＋to** *do*〉「**O に～するよう頼む**」が【**受動**】を表す過去分詞になっている。asked ～ problem が people

111

を修飾。

☑ while puzzling … の部分は，while they were puzzling … と補う。**時・条件・譲歩の副詞節中の〈S＋be 動詞〉は省略可。**

☑ **puzzling through a logical problem** は，puzzle が自動詞で「頭を悩ます」の意味なので，直訳すれば「**論理問題を通じて頭を悩ませる**」となる。ここでは puzzle through を「**頭を悩ませながら論理問題を解く**」を意味する句動詞と解釈した。

☑ **be likely to _do_** は「**～しそうだ，～する可能性が高い**」。**twice as … as ～**で「**～の２倍…**」。ここでは**比較対象を表す as ～ が省略**されている。実験の結果を示す部分なので，省略された比較対象は「目を動かすよう求められていない人々に比べて」ということになる。

問2

第２段落第１，２文(12 ～ 17 行目)の流れを確認しよう。

(1) まず，第１文前半(12 ～ 13 行目)は次のようになっている。

> The term most often used to describe **this new model of mind** is "embodied cognition," …

this new model of mind「この新しい精神のモデル」を表す用語が embodied cognition「身体化(された)認知」であるとしている。なお，model とは，「(理論の説明のために単純化された)モデル」のことである。また，this new model of mind は第１段落第２文の２つ目の that(4 行目)以下を指し，第３～５文(4 ～ 11 行目)はいずれも具体例となっている。

(2) 続いて第２段落第１文後半(13 ～ 15 行目)は次のとおりである。

> … and **its** champions believe **it** will open up entire new avenues for understanding — and enhancing — the abilities of the human mind.

its も it も，ともに this new model of mind を指すと考えられる。「このモデルの支持者は，このモデルによって新たな道が開かれると考えている」という内容。

(3) これを受けた第2文(15 〜 17行目)は次のとおりである。

> Some educators see in **it** a new paradigm for teaching children, one that privileges movement and simulation over reading, writing, and reciting.

　文構造は，**Some educators が S，see が V，a new paradigm for teaching children が O** である。その後の **one は a paradigm の代用**で，**a new paradigm と同格**になっている。

(4) 以上により，この第2段落では「この新しい精神のモデル」の有用性を論じていることがわかり，これが段落の主題である。下線部 it は，同一指示と考えられる its と it が直前の文にあることや，設問の「5語」という指示もヒントに考えると，this new model of mind(12 〜 13行目)が正解である。

問3

〈 <u>what's going on</u> (inside the brain)〉
　S 関代　　V

(in large part) <u>may depend on</u>
　　　　　　　　　　V

　　　　　　　　〈 <u>what's going on</u> (in the body 〔 as a whole 〕)〉,
　　　　　　O①関代or疑　　V

　　　　　　　　and
　　　　　　　　等接

　　　　　　　　〈 <u>how</u> that body <u>is situated</u> (in its environment)〉
　　　　　　O②関副or疑　S　　V

以下のポイントをおさえよう！

- ☑ **what's ... brain が S，may depend on が V。depend on は他動詞扱いの句動詞で，what's ... whole と how ... environment が O。**

- ☑ **go on は「起こる，進行する」の意味。**

- ☑ **in large part は「大いに，主として」**(≒ largely)の意味で，V(depend on)を修飾する。

- ☑ **depend on 〜 は「〜に頼る，依存する」**の意味もあるが，これは，ふつう人が S の場合。**物事が S の場合は「〜次第だ，〜によって決まる，〜に左**

113

右される」の意味。

- ☑ **what's going on in the body as a whole** は what を関係代名詞と見るなら「身体全体で起こっていること」の意味。what を疑問代名詞と見るなら「身体全体で何が起こっているか」の意味。
- ☑ **as a whole** は名詞の後に置き，「**〜全般，〜全体**」の意味。in general で書き換え可。
- ☑ **how that body is situated in its environment** は how を関係副詞と見るなら「その身体が環境の中で位置する方法」の意味。how を疑問副詞と見るなら「その身体が環境の中でどのように位置するか」の意味。

問4

(**if** we didn't walk upright **or** weren't warm-blooded),
 従接 S   V①   等接 V②   C

we might understand these concepts (totally differently)
 S   V   O

以下のポイントをおさえよう！

☑ 仮定法過去のパターン。

If ＋ S₁ ＋動詞の過去形〜，S₂ ＋助動詞の過去形＋*do* ...
「(今)S₁ が〜するなら，S₂ は…するだろう」

- ☑ **upright** は副詞で「**垂直に**」。**walk upright** で「**直立歩行する**」の意味。
- ☑ **warm-blooded** は「**(動物が)恒温の**」の意味(⇔ cold-blooded)。

問5

human beings don't really process information
 S   V   O

(the way computers do),
 従接   S   V

〈the way＋S＋V〉は，これ全体が名詞の働きの場合は「SがVするやり方，方法」の意味(＝how＋S＋V)，**副詞の働きの場合は「SがVするように」の意味**(＝as＋S＋V)。ここでは後者の副詞の働き。

例 I don't like **the way** he talks to me.

「私は彼の私に対する話し方が好きではない」

(= I don't like **how** he talks to me.)

※ the way 以下が動詞 like に対する O になっているので，**名詞の働き**。

例 You should do it **the way** he did it.

「あなたは彼がしたようにやるべきだ」

(= You should do it **as** he did it.)

※ the way 以下が動詞 do を修飾しているので，**副詞の働き**。

問6

... to (**ア**) patients recover lost skills after a stroke or other brain injury.

直後に〈patients(O) + recover(原形)〉のパターンが続く。この形をとれるのは，選択肢の中で help のみ。help は〈**help＋O＋to _do_**〉で「**O が～するのを助ける**」の意味だが，to は省略可能なので，〈**help＋O＋_do_**〉の形も可。

この時点で選択肢は②⑤⑥に絞れる。

If you want to (**イ**) a computer to play chess, ...

前述のように，help も〈help + O + to _do_〉のパターンがあるが，既に(**ア**)に入れた。ほかの選択肢では teach が〈**teach＋O＋to _do_**〉のパターンをとって，「**O に～すること[やり方]を教える**」の意味になる。

この時点で正解は⑥とわかるが，(**ウ**) describe，(**エ**) contest も念のため確認。

... head-shrinkers through the ages have tended to enlist the high-tech of their day to (**ウ**) the human cognitive system ...

「人間の認知体系を説明するために…」と考えて不自然さはない。**describe** は「**～を説明する，～を描写する，～を言い表す**」の意味。

In the 1980s, however, a group of scholars began to (**エ**) this approach.

contest は自動詞で使うと「競争する」の意味で，日本語の「コンテスト」に近い意味。**他動詞で使うと「〜に反論する」の意味**となる。この文では this approach が O になっており，他動詞として使われている。**approach** は「**(研究などの)手法，取り組み方**」の意味。this approach は前の第9段落(63〜68行目)にあった，デカルトによる精神と肉体を分離する考え方を受け継いだ新バージョンのモデルを指している。

それでは次に，段落ごとに詳しく見ていこう。 54 - 63

第1段落

[1]**The brain is often envisioned as something like a**
→ p.117 文構造Check!
computer, and the body as its all-purpose tool. [2]But a growing body of new research suggests that something more collaborative is going on — that we think not just with our brains, but with our bodies. [3]A recent series of studies has shown that children can solve math problems better if they are told to use their hands while thinking. [4]Another recent study suggested that stage actors remember their lines better when they are moving. [5]And in one study published last year, a group of people asked to move their eyes in a specific pattern while puzzling through a logical problem were twice as likely to solve it.

訳 [1]脳はコンピュータのようなものとして，身体はその万能な道具として，思い描かれることが多い。[2]しかし，ますます多くの新たな一群の研究が示唆するように，もっと共同作業的な何かが進行しているようである。つまり，我々は脳のみならず身体も使って思考しているのだ。[3]最近の一連の研究により，子供たちは考えながら手を使うように言われた場合に，数学の問題をよりうまく解くことができるとわかった。[4]さらにほかの最近の研究が示唆するところによれば，舞台役者は動いているときのほうが台詞(せりふ)をよりよく覚える。[5]そして，昨年発表されたある研究では，頭を悩ませながら論理問題を解いているときに，一定のパターンで目を動かすよう求められたグループの人々は，問題を解ける可能性が2倍高かった。

語句

envision	動	思い描く，想像する
all-purpose	形	あらゆる用途に利用できる，万能な
body	名	集まり，固まり
▶ **a body of ～**		一群の～，一連の～
suggest	動	示唆する
collaborative	形	協力的な，共同の
go on	熟	起こる，進行する
not just A but (also) B	熟	A だけではなく B も

a series of ～	熟	一連の～
line	名	台詞
publish	動	公表する，発表する
specific	形	特定の，一定の
puzzle	動	頭を悩ます，考え込む
logical	形	論理(学)の
be likely to do	熟	～しそうだ，～する可能性が高い

文構造Check!

The brain [S] is often envisioned [V] (as something 〔 like a computer 〕),

and [等接]

the body [S] ← is often envisioned [V] 省略 (as its all-purpose tool).

▶ the body の後に is often envisioned の省略がある。以下のように考える。

The brain	is often envisioned	as something like a computer,	and
the body	*is often envisioned*	as its all-purpose tool.	

第2段落

¹The term most often used to describe this new model of mind is "embodied cognition," and its champions believe it will open up entire new avenues for understanding — and enhancing — the abilities of the human mind. ²**Some educators see in it a new paradigm for** →p.119 文構造Check! **teaching children, one that privileges movement and simulation over reading, writing, and reciting.** ³Specialists in

rehabilitative medicine could potentially use the emerging findings to help patients recover lost skills after a stroke or other brain injury. ⁴The greatest impact, however, has been in the field of neuroscience itself, where embodied cognition threatens age-old distinctions — not only between brain and body, but between perceiving and thinking, thinking and acting, even between reason and instinct — on which the traditional idea of the mind has been built.

訳 ¹この新しい精神のモデルを説明するのに最もよく使われる用語が「身体化（された）認知」であり，その支持者たちは，これにより人間の精神の持つさまざまな能力を理解し，そしてそれを高めるための完全に新たな道が切り開かれると考えている。²教育者の中には，その中に子供を教育するための新たな理論的枠組を見る者もおり，それは，読むこと，書くこと，朗読することよりも，動作や模倣を特別に重視する理論的枠組である。³リハビリ医療の専門家は，この新たな知見を利用し，患者が脳卒中やその他脳の損傷の後に失われた能力を回復するのを助けることができる可能性がある。⁴しかし，最も大きな影響は，まさに神経科学の分野においてである。そこでは，身体化された認知が，昔ながらの区別を脅かしているのだ。その区別とは，脳と身体のみならず，知覚と思考，思考と行動，さらには理性と本能といったものであり，伝統的な精神の考え方はこれらを土台に築き上げられてきたのである。

語句

term	名	用語
describe	動	説明する，言い表す
embody	動	身体化する
cognition	名	認知
▶ embodied cognition		身体化（された）認知
champion	名	擁護者，支持者
open up ~	熟	～（可能性など）を開く，～のきっかけとなる
entire	形	全くの，完全な
avenue	名	手段，方法
enhance	動	高める，向上させる
educator	名	教育者
paradigm	名	パラダイム，理論的枠組
privilege	動	特権を与える，特別扱いする
movement	名	動作，動き
simulation	名	まねること，疑似体験
recite	動	朗読する，暗唱する
rehabilitative	形	リハビリの
medicine	名	医学，医療
potentially	副	潜在的に，可能性として
emerging	形	新たに出現した，新進の
stroke	名	（脳）卒中
injury	名	損傷
neuroscience	名	神経科学
threaten	動	脅かす
age-old	形	長年にわたる，ずっと昔からの
distinction	名	区別
perceive	動	知覚する
reason	名	理性
instinct	名	本能

文構造Check!

Some educators see (in it)
　　　　S　　　V

```
┌ a new paradigm 〔 for teaching children 〕,
同            O
格
└ one 〔 that privileges movement and simulation
         関代   V        O

    ( over reading, writing, and reciting )〕.
      ①        ②    等接   ③
```

▶ Some educators が S，see が V，a new paradigm が O。in it が挿入されているせいで V と O が離れている。one は〈a＋名詞〉の代わりをする代名詞であり，ここでは a paradigm の代用。one の前のカンマは【同格】を表し，後の that は関係代名詞。動詞 privilege は「特別扱いをする，特権を与える」，前置詞 over は「～を超えて，～の上位に，～に優先して」の意味。よって，privilege A over B で「B より A を特別扱いする，優先的に扱う」という意味に解釈できる。

第3段落

[1]"It's a revolutionary idea," says Shaun Gallagher, the director of the cognitive science program at the University of Central Florida. [2]"In the embodied view, if you're going to explain cognition it's not enough just to look inside the brain. [3]In any particular instance, what's going on inside the brain in large part may depend on what's going on in the body as a whole, and how that body is situated in its environment."

語句

revolutionary	形	革命的な，画期的な	instance	名	例，実例
director	名	責任者，指導者	in large part	熟	主に，大いに
cognitive	形	認知の，認識の	as a whole	熟	～全体，～全般
particular	形	特定の	situate	動	置く，位置づける

第 4 段落

Or, as the motto of the University of Wisconsin's Laboratory of
Embodied Cognition puts it, *Ago ergo cogito*: "I act, therefore I think."

語句

| as ~ put(s) it | 熟 | ～が言うように，～にあるとおり | motto | 名 | モットー，標語 |

※ *Ago ergo cogito.* はデカルトの有名な言葉である *Cogito ergo sum.*「我思う故に我あり」のもじり。

第 5 段落

[1]The emerging field builds on decades of research into human
movement and gesture. [2]Much of the earlier work looked at the role
of gestures in communication, asking whether gesture grew out of
speech or exploring why people gestured when they were talking on
the telephone.

¹この新たに出現した分野は，人間の動作やジェスチャーに関する何十年にも及ぶ研究を生かしたものである。²初期の研究の多くは，コミュニケーションにおけるジェスチャーの役割に目を向け，ジェスチャーが言語から生じるものであるかどうかを問いかけたり，なぜ人々は電話で話しているときにジェスチャーをするのかを探求したりした。

語句

build on ~　　熟　~を生かす，~を利用する
decade　　名　10年
grow out of ~　熟　~から生じる，~に起因する
speech　　名　言語
explore　　動　探求する，探る

第6段落

¹But today, neuroscientists, linguists, and philosophers are making much bolder claims. ²A few argue that human characteristics like empathy, or concepts like time and space, or even the deep structure of language and some of the most profound principles of mathematics, can ultimately be traced to the idiosyncrasies of the human body. ³They argue that if we didn't walk upright or weren't warm-blooded, we might understand these concepts totally differently. ⁴The experience of having a body, they argue, is intimately tied to our intelligence.

訳 ¹しかし今日，神経科学者や言語学者や哲学者は，はるかに大胆な主張をしている。²感情移入のような人間的特性や，時間や空間といった概念，あるいは言語の深層構造や最も深遠な数学的原理のいくつかさえ，究極的には人体の特異性に由来すると主張する者も少数だが存在する。³もし我々が直立歩行していないなら，あるいは恒温動物でないなら，これらの概念を全く違ったふうに理解するかもしれない，と彼らは主張する。⁴彼らの主張によれば，身体を持つという経験は，我々の知性と密接に関連しているのだ。

語句

neuroscientist　名　神経科学者
linguist　　名　言語学者
philosopher　名　哲学者
bold　　形　思い切った，大胆な
claim　　名　主張
characteristic　名　特徴，特性
empathy　　名　感情移入，共感
concept　　名　観念，概念
structure　名　構造
profound　形　深い，深遠な
principle　名　原理，原則，公理
ultimately　副　究極的に，根源的に
trace　　動　さかのぼる，たどる

upright	副 垂直に，直立して	**tie**	動 結びつける，関連づける
warm-blooded	形 恒温の，温血の	▶ **be tied to ～**	～に関係がある
intimately	副 密接に	**intelligence**	名 知性，知能

第7段落

"If you want to teach a computer to play chess, or if you want to design a search engine, the old model is OK," says Rolf Pfeifer, director of the artificial intelligence lab at the University of Zurich, "but if you're interested in understanding real intelligence, you have to deal with the body."

> **訳**「もしコンピュータにチェスをするよう教えたいなら，あるいは検索エンジンを設計したいなら，旧式のモデルでよい」とチューリッヒ大学の人工知能研究室長のロルフ・ファイファーは言う。「だが，真の知性を理解することに関心があるならば，身体を扱わなければならない」

語句

artificial	形 人工的な	**lab**	名 研究室，実験室
			＊ laboratory の略語

第8段落

[1]Embodied cognition upends several centuries of thinking about thinking. [2]René Descartes, living in an age when steam engines were novelty items, envisioned the brain as a pump that moved "animating fluid" through the body — head-shrinkers through the ages have tended to enlist the high-tech of their day to describe the human cognitive system — but the mind, Descartes argued, was something else entirely, an incorporeal entity that interacted with the body through the pineal gland.

訳 [1]身体化された認知は数世紀に及ぶ思考に関する思考をひっくり返すものである。[2]ルネ・デカルトは蒸気機関が目新しい物であった時代に生きたが，脳を体内で「生命を吹き込む液体」をめぐらせるポンプのような物として思い描いた——精神科医は昔から，人間の認知体系を説明するのにその時代のハイテクの助けを借りる傾向があった——しかし，精神は全く別物で，松果体を通じて身体と相互作用する無形の実在だとデカルトは主張した。

語 句

steam engine	名 蒸気機関	fluid	名 液体
novelty item	名 目新しい物	through the ages	熟 大昔から，古くから
pump	名 ポンプ	enlist	動 協力を求める
animate	動 生命を吹き込む	**entity**	名 実在，実体
		interact	動 相互作用する

第9段落

[1]While a few thinkers challenged Descartes' mind-body separation, it remained the dominant model up through the 20th century, though its form evolved with the times. [2]After the development of the modern computer in the years after World War II, a new version of the same model was adopted, with the brain as a computer and the mind as the software that ran on it.

訳 [1]少数の思想家たちがデカルトの精神と身体を分離する考え方（心身二元論）に異議を唱えたが，その考え方は，形式は時代と共に発達したものの，20世紀に至るまで有力なモデルであり続けた。[2]第2次世界大戦後の何年かで現代のコンピュータが発達して以降，同じモデルの新バージョンが採用された。それは，脳をコンピュータ，精神をそのコンピュータ上で動くソフトウェアとするモデルである。

語 句

thinker	名 思想家	dominant	形 有力な，支配的な
challenge	動 異議を唱える	evolve	動 進化する，発達する
separation	名 分離	version	名 …版，…型
		adopt	動 採用する，取り入れる

¹In the 1980s, however, a group of scholars began to contest this approach. ²Fueled in part by broad disappointment with artificial intelligence research, they argued that human beings don't really process information the way computers do, by manipulating abstract symbols using formal rules. ³In 1995, a major biological discovery brought even more enthusiasm to the field. ⁴Scientists in Italy discovered "mirror neurons" that respond when we see someone else performing an action — or even when we hear an action described — as if we ourselves were performing the action. ⁵By simultaneously playing a role in both acting and thinking, mirror neurons suggested that the two might not be so separate after all.

訳 ¹しかし，1980年代になると，学者たちの集団がこのようなアプローチに反論し始めた。²1つには人工知能の研究に対する失望が広がったことによりあおり立てられて，人間は実際には，コンピュータがするように形式的なルールを用い抽象的な記号を操作することで情報を処理しているのではない，と彼らは主張した。³1995年に生物学上の重要な発見がこの分野にさらなる熱狂をもたらした。⁴イタリアの科学者たちが「ミラーニューロン」を発見したのだ。これは，我々がほかの人が何らかの行動をしているのを見たとき，あるいは，ある行動が説明されるのを聞いたときでさえも，あたかも自分がその行動をしているかのように反応するものである。⁵行動と思考の両面で同時に役割を演じることにより，ミラーニューロンは，その両者が結局のところ，それほど別個のものではないことを示唆した。

語句

scholar	名 学者	abstract	形 抽象的な
contest	動 反論する	symbol	名 記号，符号
approach	名 (研究などの)手法，アプローチ	formal	形 形式的な
		biological	形 生物学の
fuel	動 あおり立てる，刺激する	enthusiasm	名 熱中，熱狂
in part	熟 1つには，ある程度は	perform	動 行う，実行する
process	動 処理する	simultaneously	副 同時に
manipulate	動 操作する，処理する	separate	形 別々の，個々の
		after all	熟 結局

パラグラフ展開　　英文全体の内容を把握しよう！

導入

第1段落

脳＝コンピュータ／身体＝万能な道具？

↕

共同作業が行われているとの研究結果（脳のみならず身体も使って思考）

①子供は手を使うほうが数学の問題をよく解ける

②舞台役者は身体を動かすと台詞をよく覚える

③目を一定のパターンで動かすと論理問題が2倍もよく解ける

主題の提示

第2段落

"embodied cognition"＝「身体化（された）認知」

→ 人間の精神のもつ能力を理解し，高める可能性が開ける

例①教育：読み書き朗読よりも動作や模倣を重視

②リハビリ医療：患者が失われた能力を回復

③神経科学：古くからの二分論（脳 vs 身体など）の見直し

説明①　「身体化（された）認知」について

第3段落

身体化（された）認知＝脳内で起こることは身体全体で起こることに左右される
という可能性

第4段落

身体化（された）認知＝「我行動する，故に我思考する」

第5段落

身体化（された）認知＝動作・ジェスチャーに関する研究が土台に

第6段落

神経科学者・言語学者・哲学者はさらに大胆な主張

→ 人間の特性は身体の特異性に由来する

第7段落

真の知性を理解するために身体を扱う必要性

説明② 身体化認知に至るまでの歴史

第8段落

デカルトの考え方

①脳＝身体に生命を吹き込む液体を送り出すポンプのようなもの

②精神＝松果体を通じて身体と相互作用

第9段落

デカルトの精神と身体を分離する考え方（心身二元論）

→ 20世紀まで有力なモデル

→ 第2次大戦後は「脳＝コンピュータ，精神＝ソフトウェア」とするモデルに

第10段落

1980年代　上記アプローチへの反論：人間≠コンピュータ

1995年　ミラーニューロンの発見→ 行動(身体)と思考(精神)は別個のものではない

テーマ解説

　心の存在する場所はどこなのか。心は脳にあると明確に唱えた最初の人は古代ギリシャの医師ヒポクラテスであった。哲学者のプラトンも心は脳にあると考え，これは脳心説としてキリスト教の教義にも取り込まれた。他方，その弟子のアリストテレスは，心臓が感覚の器官であり，血液がそれを維持しているのであって，脳は冷却器に過ぎないと考えた。

　ルネッサンス以後，合理的に物事を考えて生きていこうという近代人にふさわしい態度がしだいに形成されていった。「我思う，故に我あり」の言葉で有名な，本英文にも登場するルネ・デカルトは，人間の身体を機械ととらえ，ここから神経を通って脳に精気が運ばれ，松果体で脳と身体が結ばれると考えた（心身二元論）。

　こういった考え方は，その後の神経科学などの発達とともに支持を失い，現在では大脳におけるニューロンの電気的活動に随伴して意識が生じるという説が支持されている。

　本英文では「身体化（された）認知」が主題となっているが，これは心身二元論を否定する昨今の心理学の潮流の1つである。また，「ミラーニューロン」と呼ばれる神経細胞についても言及されている。ミラーニューロンは神経科学における近年の最も重要な発見とされることもあるが，現時点では解明されていないことが多く（ミラーニューロンの障害と自閉症の関係など），今後の研究成果に期待が寄せられている。

確認問題

1. ①〜⑩は語句の意味を日本語で書き，⑪〜⑳は和訳と対応する英語の語句を，頭文字を参考にして書き，空欄を完成させよう。（各1点× 20）

/40点

①	collaborative	形	
②	enhance	動	
③	privilege	動	
④	simulation	名	
⑤	profound	形	
⑥	artificial	形	
⑦	entity	名	
⑧	dominant	形	
⑨	manipulate	動	
⑩	abstract	形	
⑪	p	動	公表する，発表する
⑫	l	形	論理(学)の
⑬	r	動	朗読する，暗唱する
⑭	e	動	探求する，探る
⑮	l	名	言語学者
⑯	t	動	さかのぼる，たどる
⑰	f	名	液体
⑱	i	動	相互作用する
⑲	c	動	異議を唱える
⑳	e	名	熱中，熱狂

2. 次の[ ]の語句を並べ替えて，意味の通る英文を完成させよう。（各5点× 2）

① The [new / model / term / used / to / this / most / often / describe] of mind is "embodied cognition."

この新しい精神のモデルを説明するのに最もよく使われる用語が「身体化(された)認知」である。

② In any particular instance, [the brain / inside / may / what's / depend / going / on / on] what's going on in the body as a whole.

いかなる特定の実例においても、脳の中で起こっていることは、身体全体で起こっていることによって決定されるかもしれない。

3. 次の英文を和訳してみよう。(10点)

And in one study published last year, a group of people asked to move their eyes in a specific pattern while puzzling through a logical problem were twice as likely to solve it.

ディクテーションしてみよう！

今回学習した英文に出てきた語句を、音声を聞いて＿＿＿に書き取ろう。

🔊 64 65

64　　The brain is often envisioned as something like a computer, and the body as its all-purpose tool. But ❶＿＿＿＿＿＿＿＿＿＿＿＿＿＿ that something more collaborative is going on — that we think not just with our brains, but with our bodies. A recent series of studies has shown that children can solve math problems better if they are ❷＿＿＿＿＿＿＿＿＿ ＿＿＿＿＿＿. Another recent study suggested that stage actors remember their lines better when they are moving. And in one study published last year, a group of people asked to ❸＿＿＿＿＿＿＿＿＿＿＿＿＿＿ while puzzling through a logical problem were twice as likely to solve it.

65　　The term most often used to describe this new model of mind is "embodied cognition," and its champions believe it will open up entire new avenues for understanding — and enhancing — the abilities of the human mind. ❹＿＿＿＿＿＿＿＿＿＿＿ a new paradigm for teaching children, one that privileges movement and simulation over reading, writing, and reciting. Specialists in rehabilitative medicine could potentially use the emerging findings to ❺_____ after a stroke or other brain injury. The greatest impact, however, has been in the field of neuroscience itself, where embodied cognition threatens age-old distinctions — not only between brain and body, but between perceiving and thinking, thinking and acting, even between reason and instinct — on which ❻___ _____.

確認問題の答

1. ①協力的な，共同の　②高める，向上させる　③特権を与える，特別扱いする
④まねること，疑似体験　⑤深い，深遠な　⑥人工的な　⑦実在，実体　⑧有力な，支配的な
⑨操作する，処理する　⑩抽象的な　⑪ publish　⑫ logical　⑬ recite　⑭ explore
⑮ linguist　⑯ trace　⑰ fluid　⑱ interact　⑲ challenge　⑳ enthusiasm
2. ① term most often used to describe this new model　（第２段落　第１文）
　 ② what's going on inside the brain may depend on　（第３段落　第３文）
3. そして，昨年発表されたある研究では，頭を悩ませながら論理問題を解いているときに，一定のパターンで
目を動かすよう求められたグループの人々は，問題を解ける可能性が２倍高かった。　（第１段落　最終文）

ディクテーションしてみよう！の答

❶ a growing body of new research suggests
❷ told to use their hands while thinking　❸ move their eyes in a specific pattern
❹ Some educators see in it　❺ help patients recover lost skills
❻ the traditional idea of the mind has been built

解答

問1 全訳参照

問2 they realized [found] (that) they needed more people to help them (to) tag as many butterflies as they could

《 別 解 》 they realized [found] (that) they needed more people to help them (to) attach tags to as many butterflies as possible

問3 国内の野鳥観察者による鳥の営巣記録のデータが，気候変動は緊急の問題であるとイギリス政府が主張する根拠となったという役割。**(60字)**

| **問4** 全訳参照 | **問5** (1) ⑥ | (2) ② | **問6** ③，⑦ |

解説

問1

文構造を確認しよう。

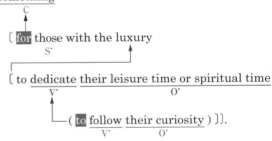

(In earlier days,) science was something
$\underset{S}{}$ $\underset{V}{}$ $\underset{C}{}$

〔 **for** those with the luxury
$\underset{S'}{}$

〔 to dedicate their leisure time or spiritual time
$\underset{V'}{}$ $\underset{O'}{}$

(**to** follow their curiosity) 〕〕.
$\underset{V'}{}$ $\underset{O'}{}$

以下のポイントをおさえよう！

☑ those は people の意味。those with luxury で「余裕のある人々」。

☑ to dedicate 以下は luxury を修飾する形容詞用法の不定詞。dedicate は「ささげる」(= devote)。

☑ to follow 以下は dedicate を修飾する副詞用法の不定詞(「～するために」)。follow は「追求する，探求する」の意味。

問2

Once these scientists identified a way to attach a tag to the butterfly without harming their sensitive wings, <u>可能な限り多くの蝶に彼らがタグを付けるのを手伝うためには，より多くの人々が必要であることに彼らは気がついた</u>.

以下のポイントをおさえよう！

☑ 「…ことに彼らは気づいた」⇒ they realized [found] (that) …

「気づく」に notice は不適切。notice は視覚や聴覚などの感覚により気づくことを意味する。realize は「考えて気づく」，find は「研究や経験などを通して気づく」の意味なので，適切。

☑ 「より多くの人々が必要であることに」⇒ (that) they needed more people

時制の一致により need が過去形になる点に注意。

☑ 「可能な限り多くの蝶」⇒ as many butterflies as <u>they could</u> [possible]

「可能な限り…」は as … as possible または as … as S can で表す。ここでも時制の一致により can を過去形 could にする。

☑ 「～にタグを付ける」⇒ attach [affix] tags to ～ / tag ～

attach A to B で「A を B に取り付ける」が直前部分にあるので，これを使ってもよいが，タグを付ける対象が多くのチョウなので，tags と複数形にする点に注意。前の文にある affix も attach の代わりに用いてよい。また，第2段落後半には tag を動詞として用いている箇所がいくつかあるので，これを参考にするのもよい。

☑ 「彼らが～するのを助ける」⇒ help them (to) *do*

問3

まず，設問文は「役割とその意義」とあるが，ここでは「役割」を書けばそれが「意義」となるので，この2つを別個に記述する必要はない。

「市民科学」に対応するのは，第4段落第3文の birdwatchers scattered across England「イギリス全土に点在するバードウォッチャー」という部分であり，鳥の巣作りを数十年にわたって観察したとある。「イギリス政府の交渉」に対応するのは，第4段落最終文で，気候変動が緊急の問題だという主張の根拠としてイギリス政府が調査結果を利用したという部分。これらの内容をまとめればよい。

文構造を確認しよう。

..., ⟨ what's revealed ⟩ is
　　　　S　　　　　　　 V

⟨ that (in many areas of study) the only way [to keep advancing the frontiers]
C　　　　　　　　　　　　　　　　　　S

is ⟨ for scientists to collaborate, not just with each other, but with everyone ⟩⟩.
V C　 S'　　　　　V'

- ☑ what's revealed が S, is が V, that ～ everyone が C。that 節内では, the only ～ the frontiers が S, is が V, for ～ everyone が C。

- ☑ keep *doing* は「～し続ける」。この advance は他動詞で,「発展させる, 進歩させる」の意味。frontier は「(科学技術などの)最先端」。

- ☑ 不定詞の意味上の主語は⟨for ... to *do*⟩で表す。for scientists to collaborate の部分は, scientists と collaborate に「主語⇒述語」の関係が成立。「科学者が共同研究を行うこと」と訳す。collaborate with ～で「～と共同研究を行う」。

- ☑ not just *A* but (also) *B* は not only *A* but (also) *B* と同じ意味。

問5

(1) 「第3段落によると, 以下の出来事はどの順序で起こったか。①～⑦の中から1つ選びなさい」

A　レイチェル・カーソンが『沈黙の春』を出版した。

B　捕食性の鳥が, 卵の殻が薄くなったために危機に直面した。

C　市民科学者が合法的に卵の殻の標本を収集した。

D　殺虫剤 DDT が製造された。

第3段落第2・3文より,『沈黙の春』の中で DDT により鳥の卵の殻が薄くなったと書かれていることがわかる。そこで, D⇒B⇒A という順序がわかる。第3段落第5文より, DDT 製造以前に卵の標本が収集されていたことがわかる。そこで, C は D より前に入る。以上により, ⑥ C → D → B → A が正解。

(2)「第5段落の二重下線部分を見なさい。著者は「科学は再び流動的である」で何を意味しているか。①〜⑤の中から1つ選びなさい」

①伝統的な科学的アプローチは，新しい状況や環境を評価する際に特に重要だと考えられている。

②今日の市民科学者は，先人たちと同様に科学の世界に大きな影響を与えている。

③たまたま科学の歴史は水のイメージが特徴となっていることが多い。

④科学者は，人類の歴史の中で何度も繰り返し発生してきた問題に常に直面している。

⑤科学者は，新しい理論を創り出すために別の職業からの発想を受け入れることに消極的だ。

「科学が流動的だ（in flux）」という表現は，第1段落第1文にある。ここでは，科学がまだ職業となっていない時代に，他の職業を持つ余裕のある人々が科学の発展に貢献したことが具体的に記述されている。第5段落では，インターネットやスマートフォンの時代になって，オンラインで観察結果の共有やデータ処理に協力する人々について記述されている。両者に共通するのは，科学を職業としない人々（＝市民科学者）の影響である。正解は②。他の選択肢の内容はいずれも本文に記述がない。

問6

①「アントニー・ファン・レーウェンフックは，自らがレンズ製造と微生物に人生を捧げたのと同様に，科学を職業にするよう仲間の市民科学者に勧めた」

⇒第1段落第4〜6文で，アントニー・ファン・レーウェンフックが微生物を発見したことやレンズを開発したことが書かれているが，他者に何かを勧めたという記述はない。

②「ミネソタ州の学校教員と10代の生徒2人は，オオカバマダラが北米からメキシコまで移動するという証拠を報告した」

⇒第2段落第6・7文で，発見された蝶にタグを付けたのが教員及び生徒であることがわかるが，証拠を報告したという記述はない。

③「オオカバマダラにタグを付けることにより，オオカバマダラの移動パターンが理解され，その数が減少していることが意識されるようになった」

　⇒第2段落第7文により，付けられたタグにより移動パターンが理解されたことがわかる。また，同段落最終文により，タグを付け続けているおかげで個体数が減少していることを人々が意識するようになったこともわかる。よって，本文の内容に一致する。

④「市民科学者がダーウィンとシェイクスピアが書いた手紙を翻訳するためにオンラインでミーティングを行う」

　⇒第5段落第3文で，手紙を書き写すためにオンラインで作業をしているとの記述があるが，翻訳をするためにミーティングをするという記述はない。

⑤「コンピュータは人間の空間推論能力を超え，手書きの文字やタンパク質を効率的に分析する」

　⇒第5段落第5文で，空間推論能力は人間の方がコンピュータより優れているとの記述があるので誤り。

⑥「ヘルスモニターは空気の質を記録し，タンパク質の折り重なりを検出し，科学の進歩に役立つ詳細なデータを提供する」

　⇒ health monitors という表現は本文にないが，第5段落第8文にある environmental and health sensors like Fitbits and air-quality monitors を言い換えたものだと考えられる。ただ，これらの装置を用いて人々がやっているのは，環境の評価や規制順守のチェックであり，タンパク質の折り重なりを検出するのに役立つのは同段落第7文で言及されている Foldit である。

⑦「市民科学者による観察は新種の発見につながり，絶滅の危機に瀕している海洋動物の行動を明らかにした」

　⇒第5段落最終文と一致。sea animals「海洋動物」は本文の monk seals「モンクアザラシ」を指す。なお，bring 〜 to light は「〜を明らかにする」の意味の熟語で，〜部分が長い場合は後ろに移動し，bring to light 〜の語順になる。

それでは次に，段落ごとに詳しく見ていこう。

第１段落

¹Over the centuries, the credentials needed to carry out scientific research have been in flux. ²Only recently has science become an occupation. ³In earlier days, science was something for those with the luxury to dedicate their leisure time or spiritual time to follow their curiosity. ⁴In the 1600s, Antonie van Leeuwenhoek discovered microorganisms. ⁵His professional background? ⁶A cloth merchant who learned to make excellent lenses to judge the weave of fabrics. ⁷Eventually, he made lenses more powerful than microscopes at that time, which allowed him to curiously examine mucky pond water and plaque on teeth and find tiny life, earning him the title of father of microbiology. ⁸Gregor Mendel filled many of his days as a monk with experimental breeding of pea plants to understand how traits are hereditary. ⁹That earned him the title of father of genetics. ¹⁰Charles Darwin was a companion to Captain FitzRoy of the Beagle with time to see the world before planning to return and become a parson. ¹¹Darwin's later days were part of a shift in science. **¹²Not only was science becoming a profession, the precursor** → p.136 文構造Check! **to citizen science was beginning: Darwin and others started crowdsourcing for data through letters in which people shared their observations from around the world.**

訳 ¹何百年にもわたり，科学的研究を行うために必要な資格は流動的であった。²近年になってようやく科学は一つの職業となった。³以前，科学は，自らの好奇心を探求するために余暇や精神的な時間をささげるだけの余裕のある人々のためのものだった。⁴1600 年代には，アントニー・ファン・レーウェンフックが微生物を発見した。⁵彼の職業上の経歴は？⁶布地の織り方を判断するための優れたレンズを作ることを身につけた布商人だった。

⁷最終的には彼は当時の顕微鏡よりも強力なレンズを作り，そのおかげで彼は汚い池の水や歯垢を好奇心から調べたり，微小な生物を見つけ出したりすることができ，微生物学の父という称号を得た。⁸また，グレゴール・メンデルは，修道士として過ごす日々の多くを，様々な特性が遺伝する仕組みを理解するためにサヤエンドウを実験的に交配させることに費やした。⁹それにより，彼は遺伝学の父という称号を得た。¹⁰チャールズ・ダーウィンは，ビーグル号の船長フィッツロイに同行し，帰国して教区牧師になることを計画する前に世界を見る時間を得た。¹¹ダーウィンの人生の後半は，科学に変化が生じた時期と一部重なっている。¹²科学が一つの職業となりつつあるのみならず，市民科学の前触れが始まっていた。ダーウィンや他の科学者たちは，世界各地からの観察結果を人々が共有する手紙を通じて，データのクラウドソーシングをし始めた。

語句

credential	名 資格，経歴	**plaque**	名 歯垢
in flux	熟 変化して，流動的な	**earn**	動 得させる，もたらす
occupation	名 職業	**title**	名 称号
luxury	名 ぜいたく，余裕	**microbiology**	名 微生物学
dedicate	動 ささげる	**monk**	名 修道士，僧
leisure	形 余暇の	**breeding**	名 繁殖，品種改良
spiritual	形 精神的な	pea	名 （サヤ）エンドウ
follow	動 従う，従事する	**hereditary**	形 遺伝的な，遺伝性の
curiosity	名 好奇心	**genetics**	名 遺伝学
microorganism	名 微生物	**companion**	名 同行者
professional	形 職業上の	parson	名 （プロテスタントの）教区牧師
background	名 経歴，背景	**shift**	名 変化，移行
lens	名 レンズ	**precursor**	名 前兆，前触れ
weave	名 織り方，編み方	crowdsourcing	名 クラウドソーシング[不特定多数の人に無償または定額報酬で主にインターネットを介して仕事を依頼すること]
fabric	名 布地，織物		
mucky	形 汚い	**observation**	名 観察（結果）

文構造Check!

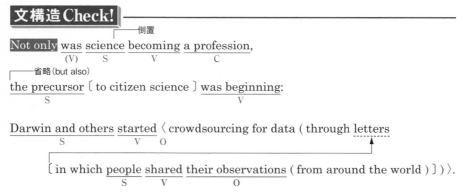

第2段落

¹In more recent history, fellow citizen scientists have continued to accomplish the remarkable. ²Citizen science has contributed hugely to entomology. ³The mystery of monarch butterfly migration had long eluded scientists until Fred Urquhart and Norah Patterson began experimenting with techniques to affix unique tags to butterflies. ⁴Once these scientists identified a way to attach a tag to the butterfly without harming their sensitive wings, they realized that they needed more people to help them tag as many butterflies as they could. ⁵In 1952, they asked for the help of thousands of volunteers and started a monarch tagging program, which eventually became the modern-day Monarch Watch. ⁶Then, in the mid-1970s, the first tagged monarch was spotted in Mexico. ⁷It turned out to be tagged by a Minnesota school teacher and two of his teenage students, which led to the discovery of the long-distance monarch migration from North America to Mexico in the fall and the return in the spring. ⁸The breakthrough was possible because thousands of volunteers had been capturing and tagging the wings of monarchs with postage-stamp-size stickers for decades. ⁹To this day people continue to tag monarchs and bring more discoveries, like making us aware of their current population decline.

訳 ¹さらに近年の歴史では，一般市民の科学者たちが注目すべき偉業を達成し続けている。²市民科学は昆虫学に多大な貢献をしてきた。³オオカバマダラの移動の謎は，フレッド・アーカートとノラ・パターソンが蝶に独特なタグを取り付ける技術を用いて実験を始めるまで，長い間科学者たちに解明されていなかった。⁴ひとたびこの科学者たちが，繊細な羽を傷つけることなくチョウにタグを付ける方法を特定すると，可能な限り多くの蝶に彼らがタグを付けるのを手伝うためには，より多くの人々が必要であることに彼らは気がついた。⁵1952年，彼らは何千人ものボランティアの助力を求め，オオカバマダラへのタグ取り付けプログラムを開始した。これが最終的に現在のMonarch Watch（蝶の保護活動団体）となった。⁶その後，1970年代半ばに，初めてタグを付けられたオオカバマダラがメキシコで発見された。⁷その蝶はミネソタ州の学校教員と10代の生徒2人によりタグを付けられていたことが判明し，それにより，秋にオオカバマダラが北米からメキシコまで長距離移動し春に戻るという発見につながった。⁸この重大な発見が可能となったのは，何千人も

のボランティアが何十年もの間，オオカバマダラを捕獲し，切手サイズのステッカーで羽にタグを付けてきたおかげであった。⁹今日に至るまで，人々はオオカバマダラにタグを付け続け，現在の個体数減少を私たちに気づかせるなど，さらなる発見をもたらしている。

語句

fellow	形	仲間の，同じ場にいる
accomplish	動	成し遂げる，達成する
remarkable	形	注目に値する，驚くべき
contribute to ～	熟	～に貢献する
hugely	副	非常に，大いに
entomology	名	昆虫学
monarch butterfly	名	オオカバマダラ[北米産の大きなチョウ]
migration	名	(動物などの)移動，移住
elude	動	かわす，逃れる
affix	動	添付する，取り付ける
identify	動	特定する，確認する
sensitive	形	繊細な，敏感な
spot	動	見つける
turn out to *do*	熟	結局～だとわかる
breakthrough	名	大発見，重大な発見
capture	動	捕獲する
sticker	名	ステッカー，ラベル
population	名	個体数
decline	名	減少，低下

第3段落

¹The modern environmental movement was also inspired by citizen scientists. ²Rachel Carson's seminal book, Silent Spring, revealed the dangers of the pesticide DDT. ³Predatory birds, such as peregrine falcons, became endangered species because DDT thinned their eggshells. ⁴The discovery that their eggshells were thinning was possible because egg specimens found in museums had thicker eggshells. ⁵Non-professionals — citizen scientists — had collected those eggshells before the manufacturing of DDT began. ⁶(The hobby of collecting wild bird eggs was outlawed in the United States in 1916 with the Migratory Bird Treaty Act, which protected migratory birds, including their nests and eggs.)

訳 ¹現代の環境運動もまた，市民科学者から着想を得たものだ。²レイチェル・カーソンの画期的な本『沈黙の春』は，殺虫剤 DDT の危険性を明らかにした。³ハヤブサなどの捕食性の鳥は，DDT によって卵の殻が薄くなったために絶滅危惧種となった。⁴卵の殻が薄くなっているという発見は，博物館で見られる卵の標本がより厚い卵殻を持っていたことにより可能となった。⁵専門家ではない人々，つまり市民科学者が，DDT の製造が始まる以前にその卵の殻を収集していたのだ。⁶(野鳥の卵を集めるという趣味は，巣や卵も含めて渡り鳥を保護する渡り鳥保護条約法により，1916 年に米国で禁止された。)

語 句

inspire	動	着想をもたらす，動機付ける
seminal	形	画期的な，重要な
reveal	動	明らかにする
pesticide	名	殺虫剤，農薬
predatory	形	捕食性の，肉食の
peregrine falcon	名	ハヤブサ
endangered species	名	絶滅危惧種

thin	動	薄く[細く]する，薄く[細く]なる
eggshell	名	卵の殻
specimen	名	標本
non-professional	名	専門家ではない人，素人
outlaw	動	非合法化する，（違法として）禁止する
treaty	名	条約，協定

第4段落

¹In the mid-1990s, citizen science was key to climate change negotiations. ²British scientists found that birds were laying their eggs earlier in the year because of climate change. ³The entire dataset, with hundreds of thousands of nesting records, was the result of decades of observations by birdwatchers scattered across England. **⁴In making the case for the Kyoto Protocol (the**
→ p.140 文構造Check!
international treaty about climate change action), the British government relied on that research to show that climate change was not a "future" problem but a "now" or urgent problem because it was already affecting life on Earth.

> 訳 ¹1990年代半ば，市民科学は気候変動交渉において重要な役割を果たしていた。²英国の科学者らは，気候変動のせいで鳥が年間の早い時期に卵を産んでいることを発見した。³数十万件の営巣記録を含むデータセット全体は，イギリス全土に点在するバードウォッチャー［野鳥観察者］による数十年にわたる観察の結果であった。⁴京都議定書（気候変動対策に関する国際条約）を主張する際，英国政府は，気候変動が既に地球上の生物に影響を及ぼしている以上，「将来」の問題ではなく，「現在」または緊急の問題であることを示すために，その調査結果を拠りどころとした。

語 句

key	形	重要な
negotiation	名	交渉
dataset	名	データセット，データの集合
scatter	動	散らす，点在させる

case	名	主張
▶ make the case for ~		
	熟	～に賛成の主張をする
urgent	形	緊急の

(In making the case for the Kyoto Protocol (the international treaty about climate change action)), the British government relied on that research
　　　　　　　　　　　　　　　　　　　　　　　　S　　　　　　　　　V　　　　O

(to show ⟨ that climate change was not a "future" problem but
　　　　　　　従接　　S　　　　　　V　　　　　　　　C①
a "now" or urgent problem (because it was already affecting life on Earth) ⟩).
　　C②　　　　　　　　　　　従接　S　　　　　V　　　　　　　　O

▶ to show 以下は副詞用法の不定詞で【目的】の意味。relied を修飾。that 節の範囲は because 節まで含むと解釈する方が自然(because 節を含まないと解釈すると，because 節が relied を修飾することになるが，「調査結果を拠りどころとする」理由にはなっていない)。not A but B「A ではなくて B」。

第5段落

¹Today, with the internet and smartphones, science is in flux again. ²Millions of people, each with their own occupation (and many too young to have an occupation yet), share their observations and help process data. ³Volunteers work online to transcribe thousands of old letters, some originating with Darwin, others from Shakespeare, and others from war diaries. ⁴People are needed to turn handwriting into digital text because automation with optical recognition software can't decipher handwriting as well as the human eye. ⁵Today, fields like biochemistry advance because people use their free time as players in online games because the human mind is better at spatial reasoning than computers. ⁶In the Eterna game, players design RNA, the blueprints that make proteins. ⁷In Foldit, a game to solve puzzles of how proteins fold, some players discovered the folded shape of a particular protein associated with

AIDS in monkeys. [8]As environmental and health sensors like Fitbits and air-quality monitors become lower cost, people without science credentials are assessing the quality of their environment, providing a check on industries to make sure regulations are followed. [9]In ports like Oakland, California, with significant truck traffic, and in New Orleans, Louisiana, with petrochemical refineries, communities organized by the West Oakland Environmental Indicators Project and Louisiana Bucket Brigade have discovered excessive exposures to pollution where scientists and regulatory enforcers have failed to look. [10]Across the world, eyes of citizen scientists have discovered that endangered monk seals were attempting to recolonize the Mediterranean Sea, that invasive ladybirds in England were rapidly expanding their range, and three new species of dancing peacock spiders in Australia.

訳 [1]今日，インターネットとスマートフォンにより，科学は再び流動的になっている。[2]それぞれが自らの職業を持つ何百万人もの人々（そしてまだ職業を持つ年齢に至らない多くの人々）が観察結果を共有し，データの処理を助けている。[3]ボランティアたちは，ダーウィン由来のもの，シェイクスピアからのもの，従軍日誌からのものなど，何千通もの古い手紙を書き写すためオンラインで作業を行っている。[4]光学認識ソフトウェアによる自動化では人間の目ほど手書きの文字を正しく解読できないため，手書きをデジタルテキストに変換するには人間が必要だ。[5]今日，生化学などの分野が進歩しているのは，人々がオンラインゲームのプレイヤーとして自由時間を利用しているおかげだ。というのは，人間の頭脳の方がコンピュータよりも空間推論に優れているからだ。[6]Eterna ゲームでは，プレイヤーはタンパク質を作る（遺伝子）設計図である RNA を設計する。[7]タンパク質がどのように折り重なるかのパズルを解くゲームである Foldit では，一部のプレイヤーがサルのエイズに関連する特定のタンパク質の折りたたまれた形状を発見した。[8]Fitbits のような環境および健康のセンサー［感知装置］，そして大気質監視装置が低コストになるにつれて，科学に関する資格を持たない人々が環境の質を評価するようになっており，確実に規制が遵守されるようにするため産業界へのチェック機能を果たしている。[9]トラックの交通量がかなり多いカリフォルニア州オークランドのような港や，石油化学精製工場があるルイジアナ州ニューオーリンズでは，ウエスト・オークランド環境指標プロジェクトおよびルイジアナ・バケット旅団によって組織されたコミュニティが，科学者や規制執行者が見落としていた，過剰な汚染にさらされている箇所を発見した。[10]世界中の市民科学者の目により，絶滅危惧種のモンクアザラシが地中海に再群生しようとしていることやイギリスでは侵入性のテントウムシが急速に生息区域を拡大していることがわかり，そしてオーストラリアでは３種の新種のクジャクグモが発見された。

process	動 処理する	**regulation**	名 規制，規則
transcribe	動 文字に起こす，書き写す	**port**	名 港
originate	動 始まる，由来する	**significant**	形 (数量が)かなりの，相当な
turn A into B	熟 A を B に転換[変換]する	petrochemical	形 石油化学の
handwriting	名 手書き(の文字)	refinery	名 精製工場
automation	名 自動化	**excessive**	形 過剰な，過度の
optical	形 光学の	**exposure**	名 さらされること，被爆
recognition	名 認識	**regulatory**	形 規制の，取り締まりの
decipher	動 判読する，解読する	enforcer	名 執行者，実施者
biochemistry	名 生化学	**fail to do**	熟 〜しない，〜できない
advance	動 進歩する[させる]，発展する[させる]	**endangered**	形 絶滅の危機に瀕した，絶滅危惧種の
spatial	形 空間の，空間的な	monk seal	名 モンクアザラシ
reasoning	名 推論，推理	recolonize	動 再び群生する，再びコロニーを作る
blueprint	名 青写真，設計図	**invasive**	形 侵入性の，侵略的な
protein	名 たんぱく質	ladybird	名 テントウムシ
fold	動 折り重なる，折りたたむ	**expand**	動 拡大する，拡張する
(be) associated with 〜	熟 〜に関連して	**range**	名 領域，生息区域
monitor	名 モニター，監視装置	**species**	名 種
assess	動 評価する，査定する	dancing peacock spider	名 ダンシングピーコックスパイダー(クジャクグモの一種)
make sure (that) ...	熟 …ことを確認する，確実に…するようにする		

第 6 段落

[1]Looking across history, what's revealed is that in many areas of study the only way to keep advancing the frontiers is for scientists to collaborate, not just with each other, but with everyone.

> **訳** [1]歴史を振り返ってみると，多くの研究分野で最前線を押し進め続ける唯一の方法は，科学者が科学者同士だけでなく，すべての人々と共同で研究を行うことだ，ということが明らかになった。

frontier	名 未開拓分野，最先端	**collaborate**	動 共同研究する，協力する

パラグラフ展開　英文全体の内容を把握しよう！

第1段落　序論

科学が職業となる前は…

⇒科学は余裕のある人のためにあった

例 レーウェンフック，メンデル，ダーウィン

↓

ダーウィンの晩年 ＝ 科学の過渡期

①科学が1つの職業に

②市民科学の前兆

第2〜5段落　本論

市民科学の貢献

第2段落　昆虫学への貢献

例 オオカバマダラの生態の解明

第3段落　環境運動への影響

例 DDT によりハヤブサの卵殻が薄くなることが判明

第4段落　気候変動交渉への貢献

例 鳥の産卵時期の早期化が判明

第5段落　インターネット時代の市民科学

例 文献のデジタルテキスト化，オンラインゲームによる RNA 解析，etc.

第6段落　結論

科学者は科学者同士のみならず，すべての人と協力すべき

テーマ解説

　市民科学(citizen science)は科学史において，科学の発展に大いに貢献してきた。市民科学の特徴や利点を挙げよう。

①データ収集の拡大
　市民科学に参加する人々が広範な地域でデータを収集することで，研究対象のデータ量が増加し，専門家だけでは手に入れにくい情報や発見できない現象も捉え

ることができる。本文第2段落の Monarch Watch はその典型例。

②科学の普及（科学教育）

市民科学は科学の理解や関心を一般の人々に広める手段として機能する。参加者が自ら科学的な活動に参加することで，科学的な思考法や研究の手法に対する理解が深まる。

③新たな視点と仮説の提案

市民科学者は専門的なバックグラウンドを持たないからこそ，新たな視点や仮説を提供することがある。これによって科学的な発見や洞察が生まれる。

④環境保護活動

環境保護や生態系の状態監視において，市民科学は重要な役割を果たすことがある。本文第5段落に挙げられていたように，市民科学者やその団体が環境評価に関するデータを提供することで，環境への変化に関する情報が得られる。

市民科学の例としては，鳥や昆虫の観察，天体観測，気象観測，海岸線の変化監視，環境汚染のモニタリングなどがあり，一般人が容易に参加できるように設計されているプログラムが多数存在する。総じて，市民科学は，専門家と一般市民の連携を通じて科学の発展や社会問題解決に貢献する重要な手段となっている。

確認問題

/40点

1. ①～⑩は語句の意味を日本語で書き，⑪～⑳は和訳と対応する英語の語句を，頭文字を参考にして書き，空欄を完成させよう。（各1点×20）

① credential 　名 ⬚
② dedicate 　動 ⬚
③ hereditary 　形 ⬚
④ genetics 　名 ⬚
⑤ breakthrough 　名 ⬚
⑥ pesticide 　名 ⬚
⑦ predatory 　形 ⬚
⑧ optical 　形 ⬚
⑨ spatial 　形 ⬚
⑩ endangered 　形 ⬚
⑪ o 　名 職業
⑫ l 　名 ぜいたく，余裕
⑬ s 　形 精神的な
⑭ b 　名 経歴，背景
⑮ o 　名 観察(結果)
⑯ i 　動 着想をもたらす，動機付ける
⑰ t 　名 条約，協定
⑱ n 　名 交渉
⑲ u 　形 緊急の
⑳ p 　名 たんぱく質

2. 次の[ ]の語句を並べ替えて，意味の通る英文を完成させよう。（各5点×2）

① The scientists realized that they needed more people [as / to / help / many / them / tag / as / butterflies] they could.

可能な限り多くの蝶に彼らがタグを付けるのを手伝うためには，より多くの人々が必要であることに科学者たちは気がついた。

② The discovery that their eggshells were thinning was possible because [museums / in / egg / specimens / had / found / eggshells / thicker].

卵の殻が薄くなっていたという発見は，博物館で見られる卵の標本がより厚い卵殻を持っていたことにより可能となった。

3. 次の英文を和訳してみよう。(10点)

Looking across history, what's revealed is that in many areas of study the only way to keep advancing the frontiers is for scientists to collaborate, not just with each other, but with everyone.

ディクテーションしてみよう！

今回学習した英文に出てきた語句を，音声を聞いて＿＿＿＿＿に書き取ろう。

72　Over the centuries, the credentials needed to carry out scientific research ❶＿＿＿＿＿＿＿＿＿＿＿. Only recently has science become an occupation. In earlier days, science was something for those with the luxury to dedicate their leisure time or spiritual time ❷＿＿＿＿＿＿＿＿＿＿＿. In the 1600s, Antonie van Leeuwenhoek discovered microorganisms. His professional background? A cloth merchant who learned to make excellent lenses to judge the weave of fabrics. Eventually, he made lenses more powerful than microscopes at that time, ❸＿＿＿＿＿＿＿＿＿ curiously examine mucky pond water and plaque on teeth and find tiny life, ❹＿＿＿＿＿ ＿＿＿＿＿＿ of father of microbiology. Gregor Mendel filled many of his days as a monk with experimental breeding of pea plants to understand how traits are hereditary. That earned him the title of father of genetics.

Charles Darwin was a companion to Captain FitzRoy of the Beagle with time to see the world before planning to return and become a parson. Darwin's later days were part of a shift in science. ❺＿＿＿＿＿＿＿＿＿ ＿＿＿＿＿＿＿＿＿＿, the precursor to citizen science was beginning: Darwin and others started crowdsourcing for data through letters ❻＿ ＿＿＿＿＿＿＿＿＿＿＿＿ from around the world.

確認問題の答

1. ①資格，経歴　　②ささげる　　③遺伝的な，遺伝性の　　④遺伝学
   ⑤大発見，重大な発見　　⑥殺虫剤，農薬　　⑦捕食性の，肉食の　　⑧光学の　　⑨空間の，空間的な
   ⑩絶滅の危機に瀕した，絶滅危惧種の　　⑪ occupation　　⑫ luxury　　⑬ spiritual　　⑭ background
   ⑮ observation　　⑯ inspire　　⑰ treaty　　⑱ negotiation　　⑲ urgent　　⑳ protein
2. ① to help them tag as many butterflies as　（第2段落　第4文）
   ② egg specimens found in museums had thicker eggshells　（第3段落　第4文）
3. 歴史を振り返ってみると，多くの研究分野で最前線を押し進め続ける唯一の方法は，科学者が科学者同士だけでなく，すべての人々と共同で研究を行うことだ，ということが明らかになった。　（第6段落）

ディクテーションしてみよう！の答

❶ have been in flux　　❷ to follow their curiosity
❸ which allowed him to　　❹ earning him the title　　❺ Not only was science becoming a profession
❻ in which people shared their observations

10 解答・解説

解答

問1

ブロック名	区切り方	各ブロックの小見出し
第Ⅰブロック	第1段落から第(6)段落まで	(④)
第Ⅱブロック	第(7)段落から第9段落まで	(⑤)
第Ⅲブロック	第10段落	(⑥)
第Ⅳブロック	第11段落から第(13)段落まで	(⑨)
第Ⅴブロック	第(14)段落から第15段落まで	(⑦)
第Ⅵブロック	第16段落	②

問2 人的資本へのより大きな投資と，段階的に提供される普遍的な社会的保護を意味する。その実現のためには，財源を確保する必要がある。具体的には，都市部の自治体における固定資産税の徴収を改善すること，砂糖やタバコに物品税を導入すること，間接税を徴収すること，補助金を改革すること，グローバル企業による租税回避を削減することなどが必要である。

問3 全訳参照

解説

問1

解き方としては，〈小見出しの候補群〉に目を通し，そのキーワードを探しながら本文を読み進めるのが効率的だろう。

①「地域の医療従事者」

⇒第13段落第2文に出てくるが，これは第11段落で言及されている social protection「社会的保護」の一例として，最低生活保障や保険制度などとともに挙げられているに過ぎない。しかも，地域の医療従事者の給与を政府から支給すべき，という内容で，1センテンスのみの小さな扱いなので，小見出しにはふさわしくない。

③「経済と経営管理」

⇒経済・経営管理のいずれも本文で言及されていない（もちろん，イノベーションによる産業構造の変化や，それに向けた人的資本等への投資は広い意味で「経済」に関連するが，小見出しとしては適切でない）。

④「新技術とイノベーションの影響」

⇒第1段落からイノベーションの社会への影響について書かれており，第2段落ではその恩恵，第3段落ではこれによる雇用への影響に対する懸念，第4～6段落ではデジタルテクノロジーによる産業構造の変化について書かれている。そこで，④は第1～6段落の小見出しにふさわしいと言える。

⑤「教育への投資と正規雇用の創出」

⇒教育については，第7段落最終文の lifelong learning「生涯学習」，第8段落第3文の investments in health and education「健康や教育への投資」，第9段落最終文の adult learning opportunities「成人の学習機会」などがこれにあたる。また，正規雇用の創出については，第9段落第1文に書かれている。そこで，⑤は第7～9段落の小見出しにふさわしいと言える。

⑥「インフラへの投資」

⇒第10段落第1文に書かれており，この段落で具体的な内容も書かれている。そこで，⑥は第10段落の小見出しにふさわしいと言える。

⑦「新たな社会契約」

⇒第14段落第1文に書かれている。同段落には，新たな社会契約による社会的保護・社会的包摂には財源が必要となるが，途上国では財源が不足しているという指摘があり，次の第15段落では，財源不足を解決する施策が提示されているので，ここまでを1つのまとまりと見ることができるだろう。そこで，⑦は第14・15段落の小見出しにふさわしいと言える。

⑧「地方自治体の公共政策」

⇒公共政策については本文で言及されていない。

⑨「社会的保護」

⇒第11段落第1文で社会的保護の必要性を指摘し，具体的な内容として社会扶助・保険制度の改善について第12・13段落で説明している。そこで，⑨は第11～13段落の小見出しにふさわしいと言える。

下線部直後に，… centered on larger investments in human capital and progressively provided universal social protection「人的資本へのより大きな投資と，段階的に提供される普遍的な社会的保護を中心とした」とあるので，この2つが社会契約の具体的な内容であると考えられる。この直後で財源不足がネックになっているとの指摘があり，次の段落ではその解決策が書かれている。解決策として挙げられているのは以下の5つ。

(1) better collection of property taxes in urban municipalities（第15段落第1文）

(2) the introduction of excise taxes on sugar or tobacco（同上）

(3) Levying indirect taxes（同段落第3文）

(4) reforming subsidies（同上）

(5) reducing tax avoidance by global corporations,(especially among the new platform companies)（同上）

問3

文構造を確認しよう。

(In fact,)

the traditional structure〔 of the global tax order 〕provides opportunities
　　　　　S　　　　　　　　　　　　　　　　　　　V　　　　　O

〔 for multinational corporations to engage in base erosion and profit shifting 〕
　　　 S'　　　　　　　　　　　 V'　　　　　　　①　　　 等接　　 ②

— that is,

some firms allocate more profits to affiliates
　　 S　　　 V　　　　 O

〔 located in zero- or low-tax countries 〕

(no matter how little business is conducted there).
　　　　　　　　　　　 S　　　　　 V

以下のポイントをおさえよう！

☑ order は多義語で「命令(する)」「注文(する)」「順序」「整理」「秩序」等の意味を持つ。ここでは「秩序」の意味で，tax order で「租税秩序」と訳出する。

☑ for … to *do* で不定詞の意味上の主語を表す。ここでは不定詞の形容詞用法で，opportunities を修飾。「…が〜する機会」という訳になる。

☑ engage in 〜 は，辞書には「〜に従事する」「〜に参加する」などの訳語が載っているが，通常は「する」「行う」と訳しておけば問題ない。

☑ base erosion と profit shifting が and によって並列されている。profit shifting は「利益移転」。

☑ that is は that is to say「つまり，すなわち」の to say が省略された形。ここでは，直前の for multinational corporations to engage in base erosion and profit shifting を言い換える働き。

☑ allocate *A* to *B* で「*A* を *B* に割り当てる，配分する」。

☑ located 〜 countries が affiliates を修飾する。(be) located in 〜で「〜に位置する，〜にある」。

☑ no matter how は「どんなに…しても」の意味。how が直後の形容詞 little とつながり，little は business を修飾するので，「どんなに少ない事業が…しても」となる。

▼

それでは次に，段落ごとに詳しく見ていこう。

第1段落

[1]There has never been a time when mankind was not afraid of where its talent for innovation might lead. [2]In the 19th century, Karl Marx worried that "machinery does not just act as a superior competitor to the worker, always on the point of making him superfluous. [3]It is the most powerful weapon for suppressing

strikes." [4]John Maynard Keynes warned in 1930 of widespread unemployment arising from technology. [5]And yet innovation has transformed living standards. [6]Life expectancy has gone up; basic health care and education are widespread; and most people have seen their incomes rise.

> **訳** [1]人類が，そのイノベーションの才能がどこへ至るかを恐れなかった時代はない。[2]19世紀，カール・マルクスは，「機械は労働者の優れた競争相手として働き，常に労働者を不要な存在にしようとしているだけではない。[3]機械はストライキを抑圧する最も強力な武器でもある」という懸念を表明した。[4]ジョン・メイナード・ケインズは1930年，テクノロジーから生じる失業が拡大することについて警告した。[5]しかし，イノベーションは生活水準を一変させた。[6]平均寿命が延び，基本的な医療と教育が普及し，ほとんどの人々の所得が上昇している。

語句

mankind	名	人類
talent	名	才能
innovation	名	イノベーション（技術革新）
lead	動	通じる，至る
machinery	名	機械（類）
competitor	名	競争相手，ライバル

on the point of *doing*	熟	まさに…しようとして
suppress	動	抑圧する
widespread	形	広まって
unemployment	名	失業
arise from ~	熟	~が原因で生じる
transform	動	変化させる，変質させる
life expectancy	名	平均余命，平均寿命

第2段落

[1]Three-quarters of the citizens of the European Union, the world's lifestyle superpower, believe that the workplace benefits from technology, according to a recent Eurobarometer survey. [2]Two-thirds said technology will benefit society and improve their quality of life even further.

> **訳** [1]最近のユーロバロメーターの調査によれば，世界のライフスタイル超大国である欧州連合（EU）の市民の4分の3が，職場はテクノロジーから恩恵を受けていると考えている。[2]3分の2は，テクノロジーは社会に恩恵をもたらし，自分たちの生活の質をさらに向上させると答えている。

語句

superpower 名 超大国

第3段落

¹Despite this optimism, concerns about the future remain. ²People living in advanced economies are anxious about the sweeping impact of technology on employment. ³They hold a view that rising inequality, compounded by the advent of the gig economy (in which organizations contract with independent workers for short-term engagements), is encouraging a race to the bottom in working conditions.

> **訳** ¹このような楽観論にもかかわらず，将来に対する懸念は残っている。²先進経済国に住む人々は，テクノロジーが雇用に与える広範囲にわたる影響を懸念している。³彼らは，拡大する不平等がギグ・エコノミー（組織が独立した労働者と短期雇用の契約を締結）の出現と相まって，労働条件の底辺への競争を助長しているという見解を持っている。

語句

optimism 名 楽観論，楽観主義	**gig economy** 名 ギグ・エコノミー
advanced economy 名 先進経済国	**contract** 動 契約する／名 契約
employment 名 雇用	**independent** 形 独立して
inequality 名 不平等	engagement 名 雇用（期間）

第4段落

¹This troubling scenario, however, is on balance unfounded. ²It is true that in some advanced economies and middle-income countries manufacturing jobs are being lost to automation. ³Workers undertaking routine tasks that are "codifiable" are the most vulnerable to replacement. ⁴And yet technology provides opportunities to create new jobs, increase productivity, and deliver effective public services. ⁵Through innovation, technology generates new sectors and new tasks.

> **訳** ¹しかし，この厄介なシナリオは，全体としては根拠がない。²一部の先進経済国や中所得国では，製造業の仕事が自動化によって失われているのは事実である。³「成文化可能な」型にはまった仕事を請け負う労働者は，最も（機械への）置き換えに対して脆弱である。⁴し

153

かし，テクノロジーは新たな雇用を創出し，生産性を向上させ，効果的な公共サービスを提供する機会をもたらす。⁵イノベーションを通じて，テクノロジーは新たな分野と新たな業務を生み出す。

語 句

troubling	形	困難な，悩ませる
scenario	名	シナリオ，筋書き
on balance	熟	あらゆることを考慮して，全体としては
unfounded	形	根拠のない，事実に基づかない
manufacturing	形	製造(業)の
automation	名	自動化，機械使用

undertake	動	引き受ける
routine	形	型通りの，お決まりの
replacement	名	置き換え，取り替え
productivity	名	生産性
deliver	動	(サービスなどを)提供する，実行する
generate	動	生み出す，創出する
sector	名	(産業・事業の)分野，部門

第 5 段落

¹Some features of the current wave of technological progress are notable. ²Digital technologies allow firms to scale up or down quickly, blurring the boundaries of firms and challenging traditional production patterns. ³New business models — digital platform firms — are evolving from local start-ups to global behemoths, often with few employees or tangible assets. ⁴This new industrial organization poses policy questions in the areas of privacy, competition, and taxation. ⁵The ability of governments to raise revenues is curtailed by the virtual nature of productive assets.

訳 ¹現在の技術進歩の波のいくつかの特徴は注目に値する。²デジタル技術は，企業の迅速な拡大・縮小を可能とし，企業間の境界を曖昧にし，伝統的な生産パターンに異議を唱えている。³新たなビジネスモデルであるデジタル・プラットフォーム企業は，地域の新興企業からグローバルな巨大企業へと進化しており，多くの場合，従業員や有形資産はほとんどない。⁴この新しい産業組織は，プライバシー，競争，税制の分野で政策上の問題を提起している。⁵政府が歳入を上げる能力は，生産的資産のバーチャルな性質によって抑制されている。

語 句

feature	名	特徴
notable	形	注目すべき，顕著な
firm	名	(小規模な)会社，企業
scale up	熟	規模を拡大する
scale down	熟	規模を縮小する

boundary	名	境界
challenge	動	異議を唱える
evolve	動	進化する，発展する
start-up	名	新興企業，新規産業
employee	名	従業員
tangible	形	有形の

asset	名 財産，資産	**competition**	名 競争
industrial organization		**taxation**	名 課税，税制
	名 産業構造，産業組織	**revenue**	名 歳入，収益
pose	動 （問題などを）提起する	**curtail**	動 押さえる，切り詰める

第6段落

¹The rise of platform marketplaces allows the effects of technology to reach more people more quickly than ever before. ²Individuals and firms need only a broadband connection to trade goods and services on online platforms. ³This "scale without mass" brings economic opportunity to millions of people who do not live in industrialized countries or even industrial areas. ⁴The changing demand for skills reaches the same people. ⁵Automation raises the premium on high-order cognitive skills in advanced and emerging economies.

訳 ¹プラットフォーム・マーケットプレイスの台頭により，テクノロジーの効果はかつてないほど迅速により多くの人々に届くようになった。²個人や企業は，ブロードバンド接続さえあれば，オンライン・プラットフォーム上で商品やサービスを取引することができる。³この「質量なきスケール」は，産業先進国や工業地帯にさえ住んでいない何百万もの人々に経済的機会をもたらす。⁴スキルに対する需要の変化は，その同じ人々にも及んでいる。⁵自動化は，先進経済国でも新興経済国でも，高次の認知スキルに対する報奨金を高めている。

語句

platform marketplace 名
プラットフォーム・マーケットプレイス（異なる事業者が商品やサービスを提供し，消費者がそれらを購入または利用できるオンライン・プラットフォームの形態）

scale without mass 名
質量なきスケール（従来のビジネスモデルや製造プロセスに比べて，デジタルテクノロジーやプラットフォームの活用によって，大規模な成長を実現する際に資産や物理的なリソースを効率的に活用するアプローチ）

premium	名	報奨金，割増金
high-order	形	高次の，上位の
cognitive	形	認知の
emerging	形	新興の

155

第7段落

¹Investing in human capital is the priority to make the most of this evolving economic opportunity. ²Three types of skills are increasingly important in labor markets: advanced cognitive skills such as complex problem-solving, sociobehavioral skills such as teamwork, and skill combinations that are predictive of adaptability such as reasoning and self-efficacy. ³Building these skills requires strong human capital foundations and lifelong learning.

> **訳** ¹人的資本への投資は，この発展する経済機会を最大限に活用するための優先事項である。²労働市場では，複雑な問題解決などの高度な認知スキル，チームワークなどの社会行動スキル，推論や自己効力感などの適応力を予測させるスキルの組み合わせという３種類のスキルの重要性が増している。³これらのスキルを身につけるには，強力な人的資本の基盤と生涯学習が必要である。

語句

invest	動	投資する
capital	名	資本
priority	名	優先事項，優先権
make the most of ~	熟	～を最大限に活用する
problem-solving	名	問題解決
sociobehavioral	形	社会行動(学)的な
combination	名	組み合わせ
adaptability	名	適応性，適応能力
reasoning	名	推理，推論
foundation	名	土台，基盤
lifelong learning	名	生涯学習

第8段落

¹The foundations of human capital, created in early childhood, have thus become more important. ²Yet governments in developing countries do not give priority to early childhood development, and the human capital outcomes of basic schooling are suboptimal. ³The World Bank's new human capital index, presented in this study for the first time, highlights the link between investments in health and education and the productivity of future workers. ⁴For example, climbing from the 25th to the 75th percentile on the index brings an additional 1.4 percent annual growth over 50 years.

訳 ¹このように，幼児期に形成される人的資本の基盤は，より重要性を増している。²しかし，発展途上国の政府は幼児期の発達に優先的な扱いをしておらず，基礎的な学校教育による人的資本の成果は最適とは言えない。³今回の調査で初めて発表された，世界銀行による新しい人的資本指数は，健康や教育への投資と将来の労働者の生産性との関連性を際立たせている。⁴例えば，この指数で 25 パーセンタイルから 75 パーセンタイルへの上昇は，50 年間にわたり年間でさらに 1.4%の成長をもたらす。

語句

outcome	名	結果，成果
schooling	名	学校教育
suboptimal	形	次善の，準最適な
index	名	指数
present	動	発表する，報告する

highlight	動	目立たせる，強調する
investment	名	投資
percentile	名	パーセンタイル（値），百分位数
additional	形	追加の，余分の
annual	形	年間の，毎年の

第9段落

¹Creating formal jobs is the first-best policy, consistent with the International Labour Organization's decent work agenda, to seize the benefits of technological change. ²In many developing countries, most workers remain in low-productivity employment, often in the informal sector with little access to technology. ³Lack of quality private sector jobs leaves talented young people with few pathways to wage employment. ⁴High-skill university graduates currently make up almost 30 percent of the unemployed pool of labor in the Middle East and North Africa. ⁵Better adult learning opportunities enable those who have left school to reskill according to changing labor market demands.

訳 ¹正規雇用の創出は，国際労働機関（ILO）のディーセント・ワーク・アジェンダ（働きがいのある人間らしい仕事への重要課題）に沿った，技術変化の恩恵を享受するための最善の政策である。²多くの発展途上国では，労働者の大半が生産性の低い雇用にとどまっており，多くの場合，テクノロジーをほとんど利用できないインフォーマル・セクター（非正規部門）にいる。³質の高い民間部門の仕事がないため，有能な若者には賃金雇用への道がほとんど残されていない。⁴現在，高いスキルを持つ大卒者が，中東及び北アフリカにおける失業中の労働要員の 30％近くを構成している。⁵成人の学習機会を充実させることで，学校を卒業した人々も，変化しつつある労働市場の需要に応じて新たなスキルを身につけられるようになる。

語句

first-best	形	最善の，一番よい
consistent	形	一致して，調和して
agenda	名	重要課題
quality	形	質の高い
private	形	民間の
talented	形	才能のある，有能な
pathway	名	道，手段

wage employment		
	名	賃金労働，賃金雇用
graduate	名	卒業生，卒業者
currently	副	現在(は)，今のところ
make up	熟	(部分・割合を)構成する
unemployed	形	失業して
pool	名	(労働力の)要員，人材
reskill	動	新たなスキルを習得する

第10段落

¹Investments in infrastructure are also needed. ²**Most obvious**
→ p.159　文構造Check!
**are investments in affordable access to the Internet for
people in developing countries who remain unconnected.**
³**Equally important are more investments in the road, port,**
→ p.159　文構造Check!
**and municipal infrastructure on which firms, governments,
and individuals rely to exploit technologies to their full
potential.**

> 訳 ¹インフラへの投資も必要である。²最も明らかなのは，発展途上国でインターネットに
> 接続できないでいる人々のために，手頃な料金でインターネットにアクセスできるように
> するための投資である。³同様に重要なのは，企業，政府，個人がテクノロジーを最大限に
> 活用するために依存する，道路，港湾，地方自治体のインフラへのさらなる投資である。

語句

infrastructure	名	インフラ(社会的基本施設)
affordable	形	手頃な(価格の)
unconnected	形	(インターネットに)接続されていない

municipal	形	市町村の，地方自治(体)の
exploit	動	利用する，活用する
potential	名	(潜在的)可能性

▶ **to the [one's] full potential**
(能力の)限界まで，最大限に

文構造Check!

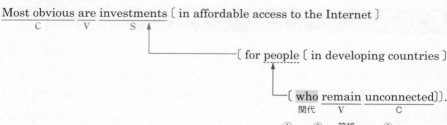

Most obvious are investments〔in affordable access to the Internet〕
　　　C　　　　V　　　　S

〔for people〔in developing countries〕

〔who remain unconnected〕〕.
　関代　　V　　　　C

Equally important are more investments〔in the road, port, and municipal
　　　C　　　　　V　　　　S

infrastructure

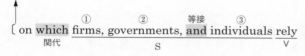

〔on which firms, governments, and individuals rely
　関代　　　　　　S　　　　　　　　　V

(to exploit technologies (to their full potential))〕〕.

▶ いずれも，〈SVC〉⇒〈CVS〉となる倒置。Sが長い場合や新情報の場合に起こる。

第11段落

[1]Adjusting to the next wave of jobs requires social protection. [2]Eight in 10 people in developing countries receive no social assistance, and 6 in 10 work informally without insurance.

> 訳 [1]次の雇用の波に適応するためには，社会的保護が必要である。[2]発展途上国では10人に8人が社会的扶助を受けておらず，10人に6人が保険に加入せずに非正規で働いている。

語句

adjust	動 適応する，順応する	**protection**	名 保護
		insurance	名 保険

第 12 段落

[1]Even in advanced economies, the payroll-based insurance model is increasingly challenged by working arrangements outside standard employment contracts. [2]What are some new ways of protecting people? [3]A societal minimum that provides support independent of employment is one option. [4]This model, which would include mandated and voluntary social insurance, could reach many more people.

> **訳** [1]先進経済国でさえ，給与ベースの保険モデルは，標準的な雇用契約以外の就労形態によって，ますます妥当性が疑わしくなってきている。[2]人々を保護する新しい方法とは何か。[3]雇用とは別の支援を提供する社会的最低基準は，1 つの選択肢である。[4]このモデルには，強制加入の社会保険と任意加入の社会保険が含まれることになり，はるかに多くの人々に行き渡る可能性がある。

語句

challenge [動] 異議を唱える，妥当性を疑う	**independent** [形] 独立した，別々の
working arrangement [名] 労働形態，就労形態	**mandate** [動] （法律で）義務づける，強制する
	voluntary [形] 自発的な，任意の

第 13 段落

[1]Social protection can be strengthened by expanding overall coverage that prioritizes the neediest people in society. [2]Placing community health workers on the government's payroll is a step in the right direction. [3]A universal basic income is another possibility, but it is untested and fiscally prohibitive for emerging economies. [4]Enhanced social assistance and insurance systems would reduce the burden of risk management on labor regulation. [5]As people become better protected through such systems, labor regulation could, where appropriate, be made more balanced to facilitate movement between jobs.

> 訳 ¹社会的保護は，社会で最も困窮している人々を優先する全体的な適用範囲を拡大することによって強化することができる。²地域の医療従事者を政府の給与支払先に入れることは，正しい方向への一歩である。³普遍的ベーシックインカム（最低所得補償）ももう１つの可能性であるが，新興経済国にとっては未検証であり，財政的にも費用が高すぎる。⁴社会扶助や保険制度のさらなる充実は，労働法規におけるリスク管理の負担を軽減するであろう。⁵このような制度によって人々がよりよく保護されるようになれば，労働法規は，適切な場合には，職業間の移動を容易にするよう，さらに調和の取れたものにすることができるだろう。

語句

strengthen	動	強化する
expand	動	拡大する，拡張する
overall	形	全体的な
coverage	名	（保険の）補償範囲，適用範囲
prioritize	動	優先する
needy	形	貧しい，困窮して
health worker	名	医療従事者
universal basic income	名	最低所得補償，普遍的ベーシックインカム
untested	形	未検証の，実証されていない
fiscally	副	財政的に
prohibitive	形	（価格が）途方もなく高い，法外な
enhance	動	高める，向上させる
burden	名	負担
risk management	名	危機管理，リスク管理
labor regulation	名	労働規制，労働法規

第14段落

¹For societies to benefit from the potential that technology offers, they would need a new social contract centered on larger investments in human capital and progressively provided universal social protection. ²However, social inclusion requires fiscal space, and many developing countries lack the finances because of inadequate tax bases, large informal sectors, and inefficient administration.

> 訳 ¹技術がもたらす可能性から社会が利益を得るためには，人的資本へのより大きな投資と，段階的に提供される普遍的な社会的保護を中心とした，新たな社会契約が必要であろう。²しかし，社会的包摂には財政余力が必要であり，多くの発展途上国では，不十分な税基盤，大規模なインフォーマル・セクター，非効率な行政のために，財源がない。

(be) centered on ~ 熟 ～を中心とする，
　　　　　　　　　　　　～に集中する
progressively 副 漸進的に，徐々に
social inclusion
　名 社会的包摂（弱者を排除せず全ての人々が社
　会に参画できるようにするという理念）

fiscal 形 財政的な
　▶ fiscal space 財政的余地，財政余力
finance 名 財源，収入
inadequate 形 不十分な
tax base 名 税基盤
inefficient 形 非効率な，効率の悪い
administration 名 行政，政権

第 15 段落

[1]And yet there is plenty of room for improvement through, for example, better collection of property taxes in urban municipalities or the introduction of excise taxes on sugar or tobacco. [2]The latter would have direct health benefits as well. [3]Levying indirect taxes, reforming subsidies, and reducing tax avoidance by global corporations, especially among the new platform companies, are other possible sources of financing. [4]In fact, the traditional structure of the global tax order provides opportunities for multinational corporations to engage in base erosion and profit shifting — that is, some firms allocate more profits to affiliates located in zero- or low-tax countries no matter how little business is conducted there. [5]By some estimates, on average, 50 percent of the total foreign income of multinationals is reported in jurisdictions with an effective tax rate of less than 5 percent.

訳 [1]しかし，例えば都市部の自治体における固定資産税の徴収を改善したり，砂糖やタバコに物品税を導入したりすることによる改善の余地は十分にある。[2]後者は直接的な健康効果も期待できるだろう。[3]間接税の徴収，補助金の改革，特に新プラットフォーム企業に含まれるグローバル企業による租税回避の削減も，可能性のある他の資金調達源である。[4]実際，グローバルな租税秩序の伝統的な構造は，多国籍企業が税源の浸食と利益移転を行う機会を提供している。つまり，一部の企業は，どれほど少ない事業しか行われていない場合でも，無課税または低税率の国にある関連会社により多くの利益を配分するのだ。[5]いくつかの推計によると，多国籍企業の海外所得総額の平均50％は，実効税率が5％未満の地域で申告されている。

語句

room	名 余地
▶ **room for improvement**　改善の余地	
property tax	名 固定資産税
municipality	名 自治体，市町村当局
indirect tax	名 間接税
reform	動 改革する，改善する
subsidy	名 補助金，助成金
tax avoidance	名 （合法的な）課税逃れ，納税回避
corporation	名 （大）企業
financing	名 資金調達
multinational	形 多国籍の　名 多国籍企業
engage in ~	熟 ～に従事する，～を行う
erosion	名 浸食
profit shifting	名 利益移転
that is	熟 つまり，すなわち
allocate	動 割り当てる，配分する
▶ **allocate _A_ to _B_**　A を B に割り当てる	
affiliate	名 子会社，関連会社
estimate	名 見積もり，概算
effective	形 （名目ではなく）実際の
▶ **effective tax rate**　実効税率	

第 16 段落

¹Emerging economies are in the middle of a technological shift that is bringing change to the nature of work. ²Whatever the future holds, investment in human capital is a no-regrets policy that prepares people for the challenges ahead.

訳 ¹ 新興経済国は，仕事の性質に変化をもたらしている技術的転換の最中にある。² 将来に何があろうとも，人的資本への投資は，人々をこの先の課題に向けて準備させる後悔のない政策である。

語句

in the middle of ~	熟 ～の最中で，～の半ばで
shift	名 変化，転換
hold	動 （内容などを）含む
no-regrets	形 後悔のない
prepare	動 準備させる，覚悟させる
▶ **prepare _A_ for _B_**　A に B の準備をさせる	

第1・2段落　イノベーションの影響

- － 失業率悪化
- ＋ 生活水準向上

具体化

第3段落　テクノロジーが雇用に与える影響への懸念

↕

第4段落　テクノロジーは新たな雇用を創出
第5・6段落　テクノロジーによるビジネスモデルの変化

第7段落
人的資本への投資
第8段落
健康・教育への投資
第9段落
正規雇用の創出

第10段落
インフラへの投資

第11段落
社会的保護の必要性
　　　　↓　具体化
第12段落
最低生活保障←社会保険
第13段落
ベーシックインカム

第14段落　新たな社会契約の必要性
中心：①人的資本への投資（**第7～9段落**）②社会的保護（**第11～13段落**）
⇒財源が必要
⇒**第15段落**　財源確保の方法

第16段落　結論
テクノロジーにより仕事の性質が変化⇒人的資本への投資が必要

164

テーマ解説

　今回の英文の出典は世界銀行が発表している「世界開発報告（WDR：World Development Report）」2019 年版。WDR は世界銀行のウェブサイト上にあり（https://www.worldbank.org/），日本語版もあるので，読んでみてほしい。テーマは The Changing Nature of Work「仕事の本質の変化」とあるが，本文を読めばわかるように，テクノロジーの進歩が雇用や経済構造に与える影響について書かれている。このテーマについてポイントを整理しておこう。

①雇用の創出と破壊

　テクノロジーの進歩は新しい産業や職種を生み出す一方で，一部の古い職種を消滅させる場合がある。例えば，自動化により，工場の労働者や一部の事務作業者の需要が減少することが考えられる。しかし，同時にテクノロジーに関連する新たな職種やスキルの需要も増加する。

②要求されるスキルの変化

　テクノロジーの進歩は高度なデジタルスキルやコンピュータサイエンスの知識を必要とする職種の需要を増加させる。これに対応できない人々は雇用機会を失う可能性が高まる。一方で，デジタルスキルを持つ人々は労働市場において競争力を維持しやすくなる。

③新たな産業の成長

　テクノロジーの発展により，新たな産業が成長し，雇用を生み出す。例えば，クラウドコンピューティング，人工知能，バイオテクノロジーなどの分野が急成長しており，多くの新しい仕事が創出され，新たなビジネスモデルが台頭している。

④グローバルな労働市場

　テクノロジーによって仕事がオンラインで遠隔地から行えるようになり，労働市場がグローバル化した。これにより，企業は世界中から人材を採用でき，労働市場の競争が激化する結果となる。

⑤収入格差

　テクノロジーの進歩は高度なスキルを持つ労働者には高い収入をもたらし，一方で低賃金労働者には収入格差を広げる可能性がある。これにより社会的な不平等が増大することが懸念されている。

⑥教育と再訓練

　テクノロジーの変化に適応するために，労働者は継続的な教育とスキルの再訓練を受ける必要がある。政府や企業は，既に学校教育を終えている労働者に対する新たな教育プログラムを提供することが求められる。

確認問題

1. ①～⑩は語句の意味を日本語で書き，⑪～⑳は和訳と対応する英語の語句を，頭文字を参考にして書き，空欄を完成させよう。（各1点×20）

① notable 　　　　　　　　形 _____

② competition 　　　　　　名 _____

③ revenue 　　　　　　　　名 _____

④ cognitive 　　　　　　　形 _____

⑤ make the most of ～ 　熟 _____

⑥ outcome 　　　　　　　　名 _____

⑦ highlight 　　　　　　　動 _____

⑧ affordable 　　　　　　　形 _____

⑨ burden 　　　　　　　　名 _____

⑩ fiscal 　　　　　　　　　形 _____

⑪ [r] 　　　形 型通りの，お決まりの

⑫ [c] 　　　名 資本

⑬ [i] 　　　名 投資

⑭ [a] 　　　形 年間の，毎年の

⑮ [u] 　　　形 失業して

⑯ [v] 　　　形 自発的な，任意の

⑰ [s] 　　　動 強化する

⑱ [o] 　　　形 全体的な

⑲ [e] 　　　動 高める，向上させる

⑳ [e] 　　　名 見積もり，概算

2. 次の[ ]の語句を並べ替えて，意味の通る英文を完成させよう。（各5点×2）

① A societal minimum [of / independent / support / that / employment / provides] is one option.

　　雇用とは別の支援を提供する社会的最低生活保障は，1つの選択肢である。

② [for / that / technology / benefit / offers / societies / to / from / the / potential], they would need a new social contract.

技術がもたらす可能性から社会が利益を得るためには，新たな社会契約が必要であろう。

3. 次の英文を和訳してみよう。（10 点）

Equally important are more investments in the road, port, and municipal infrastructure on which firms, governments, and individuals rely to exploit technologies to their full potential.

＊ municipal「地方自治体の」　＊ exploit「利用する」

ディクテーションしてみよう！

今回学習した英文に出てきた語句を，音声を聞いて_____に書き取ろう。

89　　There has never been a time when mankind was not afraid of where its talent for innovation might lead. In the 19th century, Karl Marx worried that "machinery ❶_____ a superior competitor to the worker, always on the point of making him superfluous. It is the most powerful weapon for suppressing strikes." John Maynard Keynes warned in 1930 of widespread unemployment ❷_____. And yet innovation has transformed living standards. ❸_____ has gone up; basic health care and education are widespread; and most people have seen their incomes rise.

90　　Three-quarters of the citizens of the European Union, the world's lifestyle superpower, believe that the workplace ❹_____, according to a recent Eurobarometer survey. Two-thirds said technology will benefit society and improve their quality of life ❺_____.

91　　Despite this optimism, concerns about the future remain. People living in advanced economies are anxious about the sweeping ❻_____ _____. They hold a view that rising inequality, compounded by the advent of the gig economy (in which organizations contract with independent workers for short-term engagements), is encouraging a race to the bottom in working conditions.

確認問題の答

1. ①注目すべき，顕著な　②競争　③歳入，収益　④認知の
　⑤〜を最大限に活用する　⑥結果，成果　⑦目立たせる，強調する　⑧手頃な(価格の)
　⑨負担　⑩財政的な　⑪ routine　⑫ capital　⑬ investment　⑭ annual　⑮ unemployed
　⑯ voluntary　⑰ strengthen　⑱ overall　⑲ enhance　⑳ estimate
2. ① that provides support independent of employment　（第 12 段落　第 3 文）
　② For societies to benefit from the potential that technology offers　（第 14 段落　第 1 文）
3. 同様に重要なのは，企業，政府，個人がテクノロジーを最大限に活用するために依存する，道路，港湾，地方自治体のインフラへのさらなる投資である。　（第 10 段落　第 3 文）

ディクテーションしてみよう！の答

❶ does not just act as　❷ arising from technology
❸ Life expectancy　❹ benefits from technology　❺ even further
❻ impact of technology on employment